TECHNIQUES
IN
MARRIAGE AND FAMILY
COUNSELING

■ Volume One ■

Edited by Richard E. Watts

THE FAMILY PSYCHOLOGY AND COUNSELING SERIES

■■■

Developed Collaboratively by the American Counseling Association and
the International Association of Marriage and Family Counselors

TECHNIQUES IN MARRIAGE AND FAMILY COUNSELING, VOLUME ONE

10 9 8 7 6 5 4 3 2 1

American Counseling Association
5999 Stevenson Avenue
Alexandria, VA 22304

Director of Publications
Carolyn C. Baker

Copy Editor
Wendy Lieberman Taylor

Cover design by Martha Woolsey

H 10
. T 37
2000
vol. 1
cop. 2

Library of Congress Cataloging-in-Publication Data

Techniques in marriage and family counseling, Volume One / edited by Richard E. Watts
    p. cm. (The family psychology and counseling series)
Includes bibliographical references.
ISBN 1-55620-211-3 (alk. paper)
    1. Marriage counseling. 2. Family counseling I. Watts, Richard E. II. Series.
HQ10. T39 1999
362. 82' 86—dc21

99-32975
CIP

The Family Psychology and Counseling Series

Counseling the Aging and Their Families
Irene Deitch, PhD, and Candace Ward Howell, MS

Counseling Asian Families From a Systems Perspective
Kit S. Ng, PhD

Counseling Families With Chronic Illness
Susan McDaniel, PhD

Ethical Casebook for the Practice of Marriage and Family Counseling
Patricia Stevens, PhD

Mid-Life Divorce Counseling
Lita Linzer Schwartz, PhD

Social Construction in Couple and Family Counseling
John D. West, EdD, Donald L. Bubenzer, PhD, and James Robert Bitter, EdD

Techniques in Marriage and Family Counseling, Volume One
Richard E. Watts, PhD

Transitioning From Individual to Family Counseling
Charles Huber, PhD

Understanding Stepfamilies: Implications for Assessment and Treatment
Debra Huntley, PhD

In Preparation

African American Family Counseling
Jo-Ann Lipford Sanders, PhD, and Carla Bradley, PhD

Feminist Family Therapy
Kathleen May, PhD

iv

High Performing Families: Causes, Consequences, and Clinical Solutions
Bryan E. Robinson, PhD, and Nancy D. Chase, PhD

Integrative and Biopsychosocial Therapy
Len T. Sperry, MD, PhD

Practical Approaches for School Counselors: Integrating Family Counseling in School Settings
Lynn D. Miller, PhD

Techniques in Marriage and Family Therapy, Volume Two
Richard E. Watts, PhD

Advisory Board

■ ■ ■

THE FAMILY PSYCHOLOGY AND COUNSELING SERIES

Table of Contents

From the Series Editor

> When you are riding a dead horse,
> the best strategy is to dismount.
> —*Dakota tribal wisdom*

The gap between the reality of our professional practice and what we read in most of the professional publications seems to be widening. This book, *Techniques in Marriage and Family Counseling, Volume One*, is a notable exception. Jargon-free pragmatic suggestions about how to improve your clinical practice abound. As with all tools of the trade, the professional counselor must modify them to fit their setting and type of practice. However, the seeds for effective intervention are planted within this volume by Richard E. Watts and his collaborators.

The book is divided into three parts, allowing the reader to sample from techniques of assessment, transgenerational techniques, and constructivist techniques.

Assessment is the basis of all effective interventions. It is important to decide, as Paul (1967) stated 30 years ago, "what treatment, by whom, is most effective for this individual with that specific problem and under what set of circumstances" (p. 111). Using the most effective techniques for assessment can make the difference between therapeutic success and failure.

The second section deals with the timeless importance of transgenerational understanding and intervention. Religious and intimacy genograms as well as questionnaires and inventories are highlighted.

The third section addresses contemporary constructivist techniques for helping couples and families. Techniques such as the structured externalization interview, therapeutic gossip, and scriptotherapy are presented.

This volume does not purport to have all the answers, but it has some special activities and techniques that can be used to improve relationships. We are all aware that whether or not a change works depends on the couples and families with whom we work.

> If at times a specific activity or "technique" can be used to improve the relationship or to enhance the results of therapy, it comes forth in an egalitarian relationship as something that a therapist knows how to do and can propose for therapeutic effectiveness. Use of the activity then becomes part of moving forward in life, not a way to get to a specific place or attain a specific result. (Carlson & Slavik, 1997, p. 2)

—Jon Carlson, PsyD, EdD
Series Editor

References

Carlson, J., & Slavik, S. (1997) *Techniques in Adlerian psychology*. Philadelphia: Accelerated Development.

Paul, G. (1967). Strategy of outcome research in psychotherapy. *Journal of Consulting Psychology, 31*, 109–118.

Preface

Couple and family counselors are a creative group. They are able to take foundational ideas from the family counseling literature and adapt, modify, and refine them to create interventions that best serve the unique couples and families that they serve. This volume is a collection of just such adaptations and modifications by experienced couple and family counselors and counselor educators.

The techniques described stem from diverse theoretical models but focus on the practical use of the techniques; that is, they are practitioner friendly. The authors briefly overview the theoretical and logistical underpinnings of each technique and explain in greater detail the technique and its implementation. Part I addresses techniques typically used during the introductory period of counseling and at other times when assessment is the focus. Part II presents techniques stemming from various models of transgenerational family counseling theory and practice. Part III contains techniques developed from a more constructivist theoretical perspective.

The techniques contained herein are "general working versions" (Sherman & Fredman, 1985); that is, they do not include the specific application refinements that each therapist must make in applying them to the unique clients with whom he or she works. Techniques are "tools of the trade," and their ultimate utility rests in the hands of the counselor using them. However, there is ample room for creative refinement and adaptation to meet the counselor's needs and desired results. This book will introduce readers to several creative interventions. It is my hope that it will also serve as a catalyst to practitioners in their own creative development and refinement of techniques in couple and family counseling.

—Richard E. Watts, PhD

References

Sherman, R., & Fredman, N. (1985). *Handbook of structured techniques in marriage and family therapy.* New York: Brunner/Mazel.

■ ■ ■

Biographies

Richard E. Watts, PhD, is an associate professor of counseling in the Adult, Counseling, Health, and Vocational Education Department at Kent State University in Kent, Ohio. He received his PhD in counseling from the University of North Texas. Prior to joining the Kent State faculty in 1998, Dr. Watts was assistant professor of counseling at Texas A&M University—Commerce. Dr. Watts has authored over 50 professional articles and book chapters and one book. He is the associate editor for *The Journal of Humanistic Counseling, Education, and Development*. He is also a contributing editor for *The Journal of Individual Psychology* and is on the editorial boards of *The Journal of Counseling and Development, The Family Journal: Counseling and Therapy for Couples and Families*, and *The International Journal of Play Therapy*. Dr. Watts's current interests include Adlerian, cognitive, and constructive approaches to individual and couple/family therapy, counselor supervision and counselor efficacy, ethical and legal issues, play therapy, and religious and spirituality issues in counseling.

Jon Carlson, PsyD, EdD, is Distinguished Professor at Governors State University in University Park, Illinois, and Director of the Lake Geneva Wellness Clinic in Wisconsin. He is the editor of *The Family Journal: Counseling and Therapy for Couples and Families* and has served as president of the International Association of Marriage and Family Counselors.

Contributors

Cynthia Baldwin, PhD, is an assistant professor in the Counseling and Educational Psychology Department, University of Nevada, Reno, Nevada.

James Robert Bitter, PhD, is a professor in the Department of Human Development and Learning, East Tennessee State University, Johnson City, Tennessee.

Michael R. Carns, PhD, is an associate professor in the Department of Educational Administration and Psychological Services, Southwest Texas State University, San Marcos, Texas.

Frank M. Dattilio, PhD, is a therapist and clinical director at the Center for Integrative Psychotherapy, Allentown, Pennsylvania.

Phyllis Erdman, PhD, is an associate professor in the Department of Counseling, Texas A&M University, Commerce, Texas.

Marsha Wiggins Frame, PhD, is an assistant professor in the Counseling Psychology and Counselor Education Department, University of Colorado, Denver, Colorado.

Marsha J. Harmon, PhD, is an associate professor in the Department of Psychology and Philosophy, Sam Houston State University, Huntsville, Texas.

Janice Miner Holden, EdD, is an associate professor in the Department of Counseling, Development, and Higher Education, University of North Texas, Denton, Texas.

Alan J. Hovestadt, EdD, is a professor in the Department of Counselor Education and Counseling Psychology, Western Michigan University, Kalamazoo, Michigan.

David M. Kaplan, PhD, is an associate professor in the Counseling Program, Department of Education, Alfred University, Alfred, New York.

Robert Keenan, MA, is a therapist at the Island Grove Treatment Center, Greeley, Colorado.

Patricia Parr, PhD, is an assistant professor in the Department of Counseling and Special Education, University of Akron, Akron, Ohio.

Richard J. Riordan, PhD, is a professor in the Department of Counseling and Psychological Services, Georgia State University, Atlanta, Georgia.

Sharon L. Rocha, MA, is a therapist in private practice, Beaverton, Oregon.

Robert Sherman, EdD, is Professor Emeritus, Queens College, New York.

Johanna E. Soet, MA, is a graduate student in the Department of Counseling and Psychological Services, Georgia State University, Atlanta, Georgia.

Daniel S. Sweeney, PhD, is an assistant professor in the Counseling Program, George Fox University, Portland, Oregon.

William M. Walsh, PhD, is a professor in the Division of Professional Psychology, University of Northern Colorado, Greeley, Colorado.

Sherry A. Gallagher Warden, PhD, is an associate professor in the Department of Counseling, Youngstown State University, Youngstown, Ohio.

Mary S. Wheeler, PhD, is a therapist-consultant at TRT Associates, Highlands, North Carolina.

John Zarski, PhD, is a professor in the Marriage and Family Therapy Training Program, University of Akron, Akron, Ohio.

INTRODUCTORY AND ASSESSMENT-ORIENTED TECHNIQUES

Part I presents techniques typically used early in the counseling process. David Kaplan's opening chapter discusses how structured informed consent procedures can be used to develop the sense of trust necessary to establish a solid therapeutic relationship. Chapter 2, by Cynthia Baldwin, describes how the figure/ground concept from Gestalt therapy may be used to help counselors and clients gain awareness of unexpressed needs and desired goals in counseling with couples and families. In the third chapter, Marsha Harmon explains how counselors can use a Jungian-based assessment instrument to help couples appreciate their partner's strengths and limitations as well as their own. Janice Miner Holden, in chapter 4, discusses how counselors can use the Adlerian-based assessment idea of personality priorities—pleasing, superiority, comfort, and control—to help couples understand and modify sources of distress and conflict.

Chapter 5, by Daniel Sweeney and Sharon Rocha, addresses the utility of family play therapy to encourage the active engagement of children and adults in both the assessment and counseling process. In the sixth chapter, Frank Dattilio presents an exercise in which couples are asked to draw circular representations of their current perceptions of their relationship and their desires for improvement of the same. Chapter 7, by Richard Watts, explains the use of a couple questionnaire designed to obtain each partner's early recollections of the roles and responsibilities of marital relationships. Mary Wheeler, in chapter 8, describes the use of an Adlerian-based instrument that provides a quick assessment of how couples address the life task of intimacy, their level of adjustment as a couple, and how they respond to partner differences. The final chapter in Part I, by John Zarski and Patricia Parr, describes the use of pie-shaped outlines to graphically assess couple perceptions of roles and responsibilities within the marital dyad and the larger family context.

1

Using an Informed Consent Brochure to Help Establish a Solid Therapeutic Relationship

David M. Kaplan, PhD

Imagine the following scenario: A person with whom you have had a slight acquaintance comes up to you and insists that he or she can help your family with its problems. However, this person will not tell you how he or she is going to help, what will be done with the information provided, who will be told that help is being sought, or the possibilities of what may go wrong. The next thing you hear this stranger saying is, "Relax and tell me your deepest, darkest family secret."

It can be argued that couples and family counselors who have not set up specific procedures for gaining informed consent are essentially playing out the above scenario and, therefore, are setting up a poor environment for establishing a solid relationship. What is informed consent? It simply refers to the process of providing enough information about your specific rules of practice to clients so that a knowledgeable decision can be made about entering into and continuing counseling (Kaplan & Culkin, 1995).

Informed consent has been a recent focus in the field of ethics in counseling. For example, the 1995 revision of the American Counseling Association's Code of Ethics states the following in section A.3.a:

When counseling is initiated, and throughout the counseling processes necessary, counselors inform clients of the purposes, goals, techniques, procedures, limitations, potential risks and benefits of services to be performed, and other pertinent information. Counselors take steps to ensure their clients understand the implications of diagnosis, the intended use of tests and reports, fees and billing arrangements. Clients have the right to expect confidentiality and to be provided with an explanation of its limitations, including supervision and/or treatment team professionals; to obtain clear information about their case records; to participate in the ongoing counseling plan; and to refuse any recommended services and be advised of the consequences of such refusal.

In addition, the Ethical Code for the International Association of Marriage and Family Counselors (1993) states the following in section I.F:

Members pursue a just relationship that acknowledges, respects, and informs clients of their rights, obligations, and expectations as a consumer of services, as well as the rights, obligations, and expectations of the provider(s) of services. Members inform clients (in writing if feasible) about the goals and purpose of the counseling, the qualifications of the counselor(s), the scope and limitations of confidentiality, potential risks and benefits associated with the counseling process and with specific counseling techniques, reasonable expectations for the outcomes and duration of counseling, costs of services, and appropriate alternatives to counseling.

It can certainly be argued that adhering to ethical imperatives in and of itself is conducive to establishing a solid relationship with a couple or family because it shows that the counselor will not injure a family member (Cormier & Hackney, 1993). However, a thorough informed consent procedure also helps to get the counseling process off to a good start because it focuses on establishing trust.

The Role of Trust in Establishing a Relationship

Trust is one of the core values in a client–counselor relationship and, as such, is a necessary condition for establishing a positive therapeutic environment (George & Cristiani, 1995). Trust allows the counselor and couple or family to form a "working alliance" (Borden, 1975), in which all parties are invested in working toward change. This working alliance is crucial because it is unlikely that counseling will be successful without it (Nugent, 1994).

Scissons (1993) pointed out that clients do not automatically trust the process of counseling; the earning of trust is greatly influenced by the actions of the counselor. However, little attention has been paid to specific strategies in this area (Fong & Cox, 1983). Therefore, the following seven-step procedure for using an informed consent brochure was designed to be a major part of those actions that encourage couples and families to place their trust in the counselor from the start of the very first session.

Informed Consent Procedures

Step 1: Construct a Thorough Informed Consent Brochure

Providing information to clients at the very beginning of the counseling relationship encourages the establishment of trust because it reduces anxiety by stating expectations and providing data about the counselor (Young, 1992). Although there is a growing trend toward structuring informed consent procedures (Braaten, Otto, & Handelsman, 1993), many marriage and family counselors limit their approach to a verbal discussion of their practice and do not provide any written information. In fact, a study of mental health professionals in Florida and Nebraska found that more than 9 out of 10 therapists addressed aspects of informed consent with clients, but less than 4 out of 10 did so in writing (Otto, Ogloff, & Small, 1991). It is important to note, however, that a number of states, including Colorado, Louisiana, North Carolina, Ohio, and Wisconsin, now mandate written disclosure statements for licensed or certified counselors.

The oral approach to informed consent typically centers on a discussion about confidentiality and its limits (cf. George & Cristiani, 1995, p. 141). However, attempting to gain informed consent verbally can be problematic because, contrary to what we often believe, clients do not hang on to our every word and can misinterpret or disregard verbal statements we make about our practice. Therefore, it is important that counselors develop a comprehensive informed consent brochure. The following sections for constructing a brochure have been suggested by Zuckerman and Guyett (1992).

Theoretical framework and treatment approach. This section should describe the counseling process, theories, and interventions that the counselor uses. It should describe the risks and benefits of counseling (Haas, 1991) as well as alternative approaches that may be available (Packman, Cabot, & Bongar, 1994). To encourage trust, a positive tone should be maintained; clients are looking to be reassured that counseling is effective (Kottler & Brown, 1992). This portion of the brochure may be the hardest—and most humbling—to construct because it may have been a while since you sat down and coherently tried to think about the actual process and theories that you use on a daily basis. However, the effort is worth it because explaining the process of counseling is an efficient way to handle client fears and provide safety (Young, 1992). Keep in mind that if you needed surgery, it would be hard for you to trust a surgeon who could not specifically describe how and why each incision would be made. It is only natural for clients to feel the same way about counselors.

Confidentiality. Clearly stating your policy on confidentiality promotes an atmosphere of trust (Scissons, 1993). As such, this section is critical and should make clear what information stays in your office and when confidentiality needs to be broken (e.g., clear danger of harm to self or others or obeying state laws that mandate reporting of child abuse, maltreatment, or neglect). It is important not to promise more than you can do (Cormier & Hackney, 1993) because it is common for clients to test trustworthiness by telling a secret and seeing how the counselor responds (Fong & Cox, 1983).

Couple and family counselors can use the confidentiality section to include a statement about the manner in which information is handled when an individual member of a family talks to you alone. When they know the rules about what you will keep secret and what you will not, clients are more likely to give you their trust than if they have to guess.

Educational background and training. One aspect of an informed consent brochure often neglected is discussion of the counselor's academic degrees and work experience. This section is important because appropriate self-disclosure on the part of the counselor enhances the counseling relationship (Capuzzi & Gross, 1995), and research has found that the most frequently requested disclosure at the beginning of counseling revolves around the experience and credentials of the counselor (Braaten et al., 1993). The simplest way to complete this section is to include a copy of your resume or vita. Allowing the family to examine your credentials helps them make the decision about whether you are a competent professional who deserves to be trusted.

Appointments. This section includes information on how a couple or family is allowed to contact you (e.g., Can they call you at home in an emergency?), how often they are allowed to see you (e.g., Do you limit clients to one session each week?), and when your office hours are (e.g., Do you have evening and weekend appointments?). There should also be a statement about emergency procedures when you are not available (Haas, 1991). These components help clients feel that you are dependable (Purkey & Schmidt, 1996), thus encouraging families to place their trust in you.

Session charges. This section should detail your session charges, whether or not you take insurance, and when you expect payment. Whereas many counselors base their fee on a sliding scale for humanitarian reasons, you may want to avoid this practice from a trust perspective because charging different fees for different clients can make it seem as if you are taking whatever you can get (Zuckerman & Guyett, 1992). In addition, you may also want to avoid the practice of offering a first session for no charge because clients can feel pressured into continuing counseling sessions by a sales device (Knapp & Vandecreek, 1993).

Additional points. This section allows you to state any miscellaneous points about your practice. For example, it can be useful for families to read about your rules pertaining to custody evaluations if a family has already entered counseling, your unwillingness to engage in a dual relationship as a counselor and a friend, the specific ethical guidelines you adhere to, and a statement of nondiscrimination.

Acknowledgment. The final part of the brochure should be an acknowledgment sheet that can be signed and returned to you. By having each family member sign the form, there is no question that they have agreed to enter into a counseling contract and fully understand what counseling is. In addition, obtaining family signatures recognizes the interdependent, cooperative, and collaborative nature of counseling, thereby promoting trust (Purkey & Schmidt, 1996).

Step 2: Have the Couple or Family Read the Brochure Prior to Your First Meeting

It is not unusual for new clients to test a counselor by asking for information (Fong & Cox, 1983). Therefore, it is useful to ask the family to come 30 minutes before their first session to read your brochure. You may want to have multiple copies available for a large family to read. If you are in a small private practice without a secretary, the family can be told that you will be in session when they arrive and that the brochure will be left in the waiting room on a clipboard to read and complete.

Step 3: Ask the Family for Feedback

An informed consent brochure should not take the place of verbal informed consent; both are important. A discussion about your brochure communicates that you are caring, considerate, kind, and respectful (Haas, 1991). As soon as the family is seated in your office for the first session, ask if the information was clear and whether they have any questions. This provides the opportunity to double-check session fees, inquire about available appointment times, or state any concerns.

Step 4: Review Your Rules About Confidentiality

The importance of emphasizing confidentiality to clients cannot be overstated. Discussing the confidential nature of the counseling relationship and clearly defining the limits of confidentiality helps clients feel more safe in counseling. Counselors who are explicit regarding the issue of confidentiality are seen as more trustworthy by clients (Heppner & Dixon, 1986)

Step 5: Have the Family Sign the Acknowledgment Sheet

As previously stated, requesting a written acknowledgment that each family member has reviewed and understood your brochure helps establish trust because it shows that the family has entered into a counseling contract with you and that you value a caring and collaborative approach.

Step 6: Give the Family the Brochure to Take Home

After removing demographic form(s) and the signed acknowledgment sheet, give the brochure to the family to take home for future reference. This enhances trust because it shows that you want your clients to be able to refer to the rules about your practice at any time. It also allows the counselor to more openly trust the family because providing a copy of your informed consent brochure is a prudent way to reduce liability (Bennett, Bryant, Vandenbos, & Greenwood, 1990).

Step 7: Ask About the Brochure at the Beginning of the Second Session

When a family returns for the next session, it can be useful to ask whether any questions came up as they had a chance to leisurely review the brochure. This shows a continuing desire on your part to earn the trust of the family.

Conclusion

Much writing has (appropriately) addressed informed consent from the perspective of counseling ethics. It makes sense also to emphasize the ability of structured informed consent procedures to instill a crucial sense of trust that encourages the establishment of a solid therapeutic relationship.

References

American Counseling Association. (1995). *Code of ethics and standards of practice*. Alexandria, VA: Author.

Bennett, B. E., Bryant, B. K., Vandenbos, G. R., & Greenwood, A. (1990). *Professional liability and risk management*. Washington, DC: American Psychological Association.

Borden, E. S. (1975). The generalizability of the psychoanalytic concept of the working alliance. *Psychotherapy: Theory, Research & Practice, 16*, 252–260.

Braaten, E. B., Otto, S., & Handelsman, M. M. (1993). What do people want to know about psychotherapy? *Psychotherapy, 30*, 565–570.

Capuzzi, D., & Gross, D. R. (1995). *Counseling and psychotherapy: Theories and interventions*. Englewood, NJ: Prentice Hall.

Cormier, L. S., & Hackney, H. (1993). *The professional counselor*. Needham Heights, MA: Allyn & Bacon.

Fong, M. L., & Cox, B. G. (1983). Trust as an underlying dynamic in the counseling process: How clients test trust. *Personnel and Guidance Journal, 62*, 163–166.

George, R. L., & Cristiani, T. S. (1995). *Counseling: Theory and practice*. Needham Heights, MA: Simon & Schuster.

Haas, L. J. (1991). Hide and seek or show and tell? Emerging issues of informed consent. *Ethics and Behavior, 1*, 175–189.

Heppner, P. P., & Dixon, D. N. (1986). A review of the interpersonal influence process in counseling. In W. P. Anderson (Ed.), *Innovative counseling: A handbook of readings* (pp. 8–16). Alexandria, VA: American Association for Counseling and Development.

International Association of Marriage and Family Counselors. (1993). Ethical code for the International Association of Marriage and Family Counselors. *The Family Journal: Counseling and Therapy for Couples and Families, 1,* 73–77.

Kaplan, D., & Culkin, M. (1995). Family ethics: Lessons learned. *The Family Journal: Counseling and Therapy for Couples and Families, 3,* 335–338.

Knapp, S., & Vandecreek, L. (1993). Legal and ethical issues in billing patients and collecting fees. *Psychotherapy, 30,* 25–31.

Kottler, J. A., & Brown, R. W. (1992). *Introduction to therapeutic counseling.* Pacific Grove, CA: Brooks/Cole.

Nugent, F. A. (1994). *An introduction to the profession of counseling.* Columbus, OH: Charles E. Merrill.

Otto, R. K., Ogloff, J. R., & Small, M. A. (1991). Confidentiality and informed consent in psychotherapy: Clinician's knowledge and practices in Florida and Nebraska. *Forensic Reports, 4,* 379–389.

Packman, W. L., Cabot, M. G., & Bongar, B. (1994). Malpractice arising from negligent psychotherapy: Ethical, legal and clinical implications of *Osheroff Chestnut Lodge. Ethics & Behavior, 4,* 175–197.

Purkey, W. W., & Schmidt, J. J. (1996). *Invitational counseling.* Pacific Grove, CA: Brooks/Cole.

Scissons, E. J. (1993). *Counseling for results: Principles and practices of helping.* Pacific Grove, CA: Brooks/Cole.

Young, M. E. (1992). *Counseling methods and techniques.* New York: Macmillan.

Zuckerman, E. L., & Guyett, J. P. R. (1992). *The paper office: 1.* Pittsburgh, PA: Clinician's Toolbox.

■ ■ ■

2

Using Figure/Ground to Focus Treatment With Couples and Families

Cynthia Baldwin, PhD

One of the most difficult tasks for marriage and family counselors is information management because couples and families under stress often report a myriad of concerns. A traditional psychosocial assessment instrument, even when adapted for families, does not address or prioritize the unique concerns of clients. Inexperienced family counselors often become hopelessly mired in the onslaught of information in the assessment stage. They struggle with ways to gather information respectfully and hear each family member's perspective and then help the family prioritize and collaborate on appropriate goals. An idea that may be useful in this assessment stage is the figure/ground concept from Gestalt therapy (Perls, 1969). Gestalt theory discusses reasons for behavior as related to intrapsychic mechanisms, such as projection or introjection; the figure-ground concept alone, as a tool for increasing awareness of key treatment issues with couples and families, is the focus of this chapter.

The concept of *figure* as used in Gestalt therapy refers to the concern that currently dominates the focus of attention. Often the figure is the most immediate issue, not necessarily the most important issue. When a child cannot find her shoes and the school bus will arrive momentarily, the focus of attention, or figure, will be the immediate crisis and will take precedence over any other family focus at that moment. The term *ground* refers to all available topics and issues the couple or family brings to counseling, both in and out of here-and-now awareness.

Some issues apparently disappear because they are no longer important to anyone in the family. For example, once the child's shoes are located and she has caught the bus, the issue may no longer be a focus for the family because the problem was momentarily resolved. Some issues do not get much attention in the family because they are important to some individuals but are not of much interest to the majority of family members. For example, the working mother of the child who is chronically unprepared for school on time may feel anger that she has to be in charge of her daughter instead of her partner, who goes to work after her, sharing that responsibility. She may express her frustration to both her child and her partner. Her partner may say that the child will not cooperate, and because time is short, the mother may continue to assist the child in getting ready, and no solution is found to change the behavior. The mother may report that each morning the crisis of helping the child get ready is met with anger, frustration, and confusion, but no one else seems to care. No changes are made, and family members push this unresolved issue into the background and go on to the next issue that captures their personal or collective attention.

Other issues are very emotionally laden for a family and may need resolution, but family members cannot agree or do not know how to resolve these issues and are sometimes reluctant to bring them into focus. At the farthest extreme of the continuum are issues that family members hold as secrets. Injunctions not to talk about these issues are very strong, and family members may pay big emotional penalties for pulling these deeply buried issues from the ground and bringing them to light. Issues such as sexual abuse, physical abuse, family shame, and suicide hide like skeletons in the collective family ground. Although these issues may be of primary concern to the therapist, they may not be accessible and may not be seen by the family as relevant or appropriate in counseling.

Using Figure/Ground in Assessment

In a family, the figure or focus of a family's attention can shift rapidly, the lens changing with each person's input. In counseling, each family member can shift the figure by interjecting his or her perspective, making it difficult for the therapist to grasp the central themes of the family and those of the individuals. Hearing the perspective of each family member about what they want and how the family can change is a traditional part of assessment in family counseling (e.g., Haley, 1988; Satir, 1972). Although the value of hearing each member is clear, the process in counseling is much more challenging, especially to a therapist not experienced in dealing with multiple and competing styles of communication. The questions asked by the therapist can direct the focus or figure of each member's initial input. Here are some of the ways the figure/ground idea may be used and some questions that may be of assistance in shaping a session toward successful outcomes.

1. Set the focus or figure for the session. If the therapist is clear about the purpose of the session, it helps create a focus for the family: "How may I be of assistance to you as a family?" "What are your goals as a family?"
2. Let personal and family goals figure in the family assessment. "What would you like to see change for yourself and for your family?" "What would be different if you achieved your desired changes?" "How would you be different if your family started reaching its goals?" "How can your goals and your family's needs be worked on together?"
3. Summarize both personal and family goals from each family member. Summarizing can figure in both the needs of the individual and the family: "So, Alice, you're wanting to have more time with your friends, yet you are aware of how much your mom counts on you for child care, especially now that she has a new job and a new marriage. You'd like to see new options in your family develop so you are not the only kid your mom can count on."
4. Ask how personal goals can be met as family members work toward family goals. "In what ways have you already noticed your brothers and sisters acting more mature in taking care of themselves and others?" "How are you making room for Mark, your new stepdad, to participate a little more in the family activities?"
5. Ask the family to prioritize the various family goals. Each family member may see the goals differently, but there are generally themes that can be summarized as agreeable goals to all. Goals such as clearer communication, more participation in family tasks, more cooperation, and less fighting set up a general focus. Frequently, an agreed-on goal is a hopeful start. It

sets up a positive figure in the present and permits specific unresolved issues from the ground to be tested in the current figure: "You have all decided that more cooperation would be a wonderful change in your family. I'm wondering if you can give me a specific example or two of situations when you found you all did cooperate quite well. When we focus on how you have done it in the past, we will probably find these are skills already available. They may just need some readjustment to work better or more often."

6. Discuss which personal goals may be divergent from family goals. Sometimes individuals in a family believe that their goals do not match the goals of the family. The mother with the new job and the new marriage may find that she is pulled in too many directions and does not believe she can give the family the attention they desire.

7. Set up "both/and" ways personal and family agendas can be the focus. Sometimes bringing feelings into the figure by asking the family members to participate in the dramatization of the conflicting feelings can help individuals and the family experience the gestalt of the whole situation (e.g., Bauer, 1979; Jessee & Guerney, 1981; Perls, 1969; Polster & Polster, 1973). Family members can experience the underlying stressors and become aware of the roles they play in maintaining those stressors. What may initially appear as conflicting goals of an individual may be alternatively perceived as a more acceptable part of a family evolving through its own unique life cycle.

Conclusion

The use of the concept of figure/ground is one way a therapist can keep track of the focus when doing family therapy. Individual perceptions of the needs and goals of the family are naturally shaped by many factors, and it is sometimes difficult to determine which perspective should be the top priority for therapeutic change. By focusing on the figure/ground differentiation of goals, a counselor can keep track of individual goals and family goals through questioning strategies and by clearly choosing when to follow individual goals as an avenue to link back to the family goals.

References

Bauer, R. (1979). Gestalt approach to family therapy. *The American Journal of Family Therapy, 7,* 41–45.

Haley, J. (1988). *Problem-solving therapy* (2nd ed.). San Francisco: Jossey-Bass.

Jessee, R. E., & Guerney, B. G. (1981). A comparison of Gestalt and relationship enhancement treatments with married couples. *The American Journal of Family Therapy, 9*, 31–41.

Perls, F. (1969). *Gestalt therapy verbatim*. Moab, UT: Real People.

Polster, E., & Polster, M. (1973). *Gestalt therapy integrated*. New York: Brunner/Mazel.

Satir, V. (1972). *Peoplemaking*. Palo Alto, CA: Science & Behavior Books.

■ ■ ■

3

Using Jungian Type Psychology to Value Complementary Preferences in Couples

Marsha J. Harmon, PhD

Although individuals may provide many reasons why another individual would make the perfect spouse, partners are frequently chosen to meet a number of functional needs for individuals. These needs, and attempts to satisfy them, usually operate on a subconscious level (Daniels & Horowitz, 1984; Lerner, 1989). Lerner maintained that opposites do attract, that differences may indeed draw individuals together early in a relationship. However, these same differences may repel the individuals later in the relationship. She provided an example of a couple in which the man was so enmeshed in his family of origin that he found it difficult to establish his own sense of self. He was attracted to a woman who demonstrated emotional separateness and distance. She was from an emotionally distant family and was drawn to the extended family atmosphere of the man's family. Approximately 5 years after they met, the woman complained that her mate had never appropriately separated from his family; he complained that she was too emotionally detached. This situation is similar to what Daniels and Horowitz called *projective love*, in which individuals pursue partners who seem to possess qualities missing in themselves. Projective-love relationships frequently crumble when the individual partners eventually despise the very characteristics they once prized.

Lerner (1989) contended that people come from different cultures determined by family roles and rules that have evolved over many generations. Thus, individuals enter relationships with patterned ways of relating that usually intensify during times of stress. An individual's reactivity to his or her partner's differences leads to "exaggerated and stuck positions in relationships" (Lerner, 1989, p. 80). Individuals then overfocus on the partner's behavior under stress that differs from their behavior under stress. Daniels and Horowitz (1984) described this as an attribution error in which the self is positive and the other is negative. In fact, individuals may view their own feelings and behavior as just responses to the situation but attribute their partner's feelings and behavior to an unpleasant disposition.

Lerner (1989) insisted that when we work to understand and accept ourselves, we are able to manage our reactivity and take responsibility for our behavior in a relationship. If the individuals in a relationship continue to be other focused, no change will occur. Energy must be redirected from trying to change the partner to focusing on understanding the self: "As we become less of an expert on the other, we become more of an expert on the self"(Lerner, 1989, p. 209). We are thus able to know our unique selves in such a way as to better share our perspective and be less defensive because we realize our partner must also have a perspective that would emanate from his or her unique self. Keirsey and Bates (1984) claimed that "people are different from each other, and that no amount of getting after them is going to change them" (p. 2).

There has been a continuing debate about the similarities and differences among genders, ethnic groups, and people collectively over the years. Keirsey and Bates (1984) provided a brief history of attempts over centuries to delineate and describe individual temperament and behavior. They described how Hippocrates accounted for varying human behavior through the use of four temperaments: choleric (angry), phlegmatic (passive), melancholic (depressed), and sanguine (cheerful). The notion of temperament reemerged early in the 20th century when Adickes asserted that people could be divided into four world convictions: dogmatic, agnostic, traditional, and innovative. Kretschmer modified Adickes's designations—specifically, hyperesthetic (too sensitive), anesthetic (too insensitive), melancholic (too serious), and hypomanic (too excitable)—to explain how innate temperament influences behavior. About the same time, Spranger classified people according to four human values:

religious, theoretic, economic, and artistic. Freud was adamant that people were driven by the singular motivation of eros. Even Adler initially viewed all individuals as driven by the need for power but later claimed that people of various dispositions pursued one of four goals when unsettled: recognition, power, service, and revenge. Dreikers later identified the four goals of children's misbehavior as attention, power, inadequacy, and revenge.

Jung agreed with Freud regarding instincts but maintained that a multitude of similarly influential instincts motivate people. Jung used the term *archetype* to describe symbols—such as houses, suitcases, and people—that refer to universal qualities, such as love, sorrow, and fear (Daniels & Horowitz, 1984). Recent books have used such archetypes to describe men as king, warrior, magician, or lover (Moore & Gillette, 1990) and as clinging vine, star, tyrant, or turtle (Sanford & Lough, 1988).

According to Keirsey and Bates (1984), Jung proposed that the most meaningful method of understanding differences in human behavior was the study of psychological types. These psychological types are essentially preferences that emerge early in life and form the foundation of our personality. The notion of temperament was abandoned when dynamic psychology and behaviorism emerged in the 1930s. However, it reemerged in the 1950s when Isabel Briggs Myers and her mother Katheryn Briggs formulated the Myers–Briggs Type Indicator (MBTI). The MBTI, based on and an extension of Jung's psychological type theory, is an instrument that identifies 16 distinct personality patterns. The types extend across four continua: extravert–introvert, sensing–intuitive, thinking–feeling, and judging–perceiving. There are a number of texts that can explain the theory in more depth than is possible here. Figure 1.1, adapted from the MBTI manual (Myers & McCaulley, 1985), provides some explanation of the themes associated with each function. The MBTI created an abundance of international interest. More recently, books have emerged to help individuals understand themselves and others in various settings, including life/love (Kroeger & Thuesen, 1988), work/career (Kroeger & Thuesen, 1992), and teaching/learning (Lawrence, 1993).

Myers and McCaulley (1985) devoted a chapter to the use of type in counseling, in which they made several suggestions for counseling with couples. The first suggestion was to help couples "use differences in type constructively rather than destructively" (Myers & McCaulley, 1985, p. 71). Research has shown that people tend to marry individuals with some similar preferences rather than totally similar or totally opposite preferences. However, the authors main-

FIGURE 1.1
Continua of Jungian type psychology.

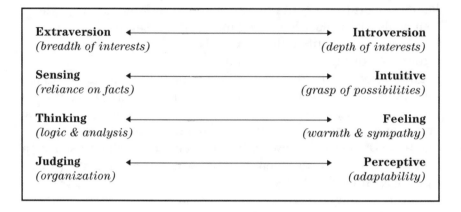

tained that happy and unhappy marriages are found in every type combination.

In the same chapter, Myers and McCaulley (1985) succinctly identified the major issues for each of the continua. The major issues for the extravert–introvert continuum are sociability and external stimulation versus the need for privacy and time alone. Communication about problems may also be difficult because an extravert tends to make decisions through talking to someone and receiving feedback. Introverts, on the other hand, tend to process information internally and later share the conclusion. The sensing–intuitive differences may lead to misunderstandings. Sensing partners may be accused of being slow and mundane but see themselves as reality based. Intuitive partners may have rapid insights but be accused of being impractical and unobservant. Misunderstandings may also occur with thinking–feeling differences. Thinking partners prefer objectivity and logical analysis but may be described as cold and uncaring. Feeling partners prefer subjectivity and examining each situation from a values-laden standpoint but may be described as completely illogical. Finally, issues of order and lifestyle emerge in judging–perceiving differences. The judging partner prefers order in planning and surroundings, whereas the perceiving partner prefers spontaneity and freedom.

If a therapist assists couples to look at how complementary preferences may help them in times of crisis or planning for the future, then individuals may recognize their personal beneficial and detrimental characteristics as well as their partner's strengths and weaknesses. Thus, the extravert would value the introverted partner's careful reflection and reticence to make a hasty decision, and the introvert would value the extraverted partner's ability to gather and process the available information to confidently make a decision. Likewise, the perceiving partner would value the judging partner's ability to organize and plan systematically, and the judging partner would value the perceiving partner's insistence on some spontaneity and fun.

I usually give a personal example to couples about how complementary gifts have been used in my research. Some colleagues have asked me to collaborate with them. As we work, it becomes obvious that I am a strong judging type, whereas my colleagues are frequently perceiving types. Through planning in the beginning, I write down the goals and time lines. They expect that I will be contacting them regarding deadlines and negotiating for new deadlines when necessary. One colleague told me that he appreciated my ability to goad him. I suggested a more flattering description was to say I provided some motivation for him. Likewise, I have found that working with others makes me work more consistently because I have to be responsible to them. The benefits for me in working with perceiving personalities is that they make our meetings fun and pleasurable; and when we present at conferences, they always make time for us to be merry and to play, something I frequently neglect to plan.

Myers and McCaulley (1985) provided a table depicting the mutual usefulness of opposite types for the sensing–intuitive and thinking–feeling continua. For instance, they suggested that intuitives need sensing types to read the fine print in a contract and to have patience. Sensing types need intuitives to supply ingenuity on problems and to energetically tackle difficulties. Likewise, feeling types need thinking types to hold consistently to a policy and stand firm against opposition. Thinking types need feeling types to persuade, conciliate, and forecast how others will feel.

In summary, although unconscious forces may initially draw a couple together, more conscious realities may be available to the partners as their relationship matures. The ability to view their differences as complementary and, therefore, valuable to the relationship comes with the ability to carefully weigh and accept one's personal strengths and weaknesses. One can then see and appreciate the partner's strengths and weaknesses. Of course, this notion is most advantageous for the couple when both partners are able to acknowledge and accept their differing personalities and that each type preference has its benefits and pitfalls.

The current MBTI is a forced-choice instrument with 126 items. It is available in self-scoring form, computer form, and hand-scoring form. Because I had the hand-scoring form in stock, I used it with clients in the past. However, this method required that I score the instrument by hand after clients found time to complete the lengthy instrument. Then I attempted to furnish literature on the four temperaments and more detailed information about each individual's type.

Recently, I discovered the Keirsey and Bates (1984) book to be more convenient for clients. The retail cost is approximately $12, and it includes the Keirsey Temperament Sorter, which consists of 70 items. Instructions are provided in the book for scoring the instrument so that immediate feedback can be provided for clients. In addition to providing easily understandable descriptions of each of the sixteen types, the book includes chapters on the relationship between temperament and partner selection, children, and leadership. Thus, the couple can take the book home and complete the instrument individually, score it immediately, and then read and discuss the descriptions of each other.

Conclusion

Partner behaviors can be viewed as either contrary or complementary. Using the MBTI with couples as described in this chapter may help partners realize that there are others who are similar to them, both individually and as a couple. The various books mentioned give percentages for each type, so individuals are aware of how common their types are. Similarly, individuals realize that their partners are innately programmed to behave as they do, rather than being strange and obstinate. Most couples, therefore, change their attitudes and become more accepting and tolerant of the formally despised characteristics unless, of course, one partner really is determined to be obstinate.

References

Daniels, V., & Horowitz, L. J. (1984). *Being and caring: A psychology for living* (2nd ed.). Mountain View, CA: Mayfield.

Keirsey, D., & Bates, M. (1984). *Please understand me: Character & temperament types* (5th ed.). Del Mar, CA: Prometheus Nemesis.

Kroeger, O., & Thuesen, J. M. (1988). *Type talk: The 16 personality types that determine how we live, love, and work.* New York: Dell.

Kroeger, O., & Thuesen, J. M. (1992). *Type talk at work*. New York: Dell.

Lawrence, G. (1993). *People types & tiger stripes* (3rd ed.). Gainesville, FL: Center for Applications of Psychological Type.

Lerner, H. G. (1989). *The dance of intimacy: A woman's guide to courageous acts of change in key relationships*. New York: Harper Collins.

Moore, R., & Gillette, D. (1990). *King, warrior, magician, lover: Rediscovering the archetypes of the mature masculine*. San Francisco: Harper Collins.

Myers, I. B., & McCaulley, M. H. (1985). *Manual: A guide to the development and use of the Myers–Briggs Type Indicator*. Palo Alto, CA: Consulting Psychologists Press.

Sanford, J. A., & Lough, G. (1988). *What men are like*. New York: Paulist Press.

■ ■ ■

4

Personality Priorities in Couples Counseling

Janice Miner Holden, EdD

The concept of personality priorities is an outgrowth of the individual psychology of Alfred Adler. According to current thinking, most persons show evidence of one of five primary personality patterns, which I prefer to label *pleasing, superiority, comfort, self-control,* or *control of others* (Brown, 1976; Langenfeld & Main, 1983). I believe that one's personality priority holds profound implications for one's relationships with others in general and with one's family members and primary partner in particular. This chapter contains my theoretical perspective on personality priorities in primary relationships and how I use the constructs in couples counseling.

Nira Kefir introduced the concept of personality priorities in 1973. Shortly thereafter, William Pew and Jacqueline Brown each further developed the constructs. In a factor analytic study, Langenfeld and Main found qualified to strong support for the constructs. Main discussed how personality priorities might be used in counseling within the parent–child relationship. In research on personality priorities in marriage, Evans found no pattern of pairings of husbands' and wives' personality priorities, whereas Main and Oliver found pairings similar to those I have observed during almost 20 years of clinical practice of couples counseling.

My conceptualization of the personality priorities both draws on and deviates from the Adlerian conceptualization. Espousing a transpersonal perspective of human nature, I believe that humans are born for the purpose of spiritual development. To promote that development, we are each endowed with particular genetic tendencies, including a motivation from birth to maximize perceived pleasure and minimize perceived pain. As these factors combine with experience in the environment, each of us develops a concept of an ideal existential condition. Correspondingly, each of us develops a primary strategy to pursue the achievement of that condition. This strategy will likely fall into one of five general categories, the personality priorities. Each priority involves certain general characteristics as well as advantages and disadvantages. Each priority also carries implications for relationship attraction, satisfaction, and distress. These implications can be particularly useful in couples counseling.

I believe that partners in a primary relationship seek counseling when their perceived distress outweighs their perceived satisfaction. My first task pertaining to a couple's personality priorities is to ascertain each one's priority. Drawing from Brown's (1976) highly developed description of each priority, I observe certain characteristics in the client's actions and words and note my own emotional response to the client.

For example, someone with a pleasing priority is likely to appear eager and cooperative, maintain eye contact, smile readily, nod often in agreement, and use words laden with emotion; when interacting with this person, I am likely to feel extremely pleased. Someone with a superiority priority is likely to appear highly alert, listen attentively with intense eye contact, and use words laden with value judgments and qualifiers; when interacting with this person, I am likely to feel inadequate or inferior. The person with a comfort priority will likely appear relaxed and easygoing; use problematic words such as *pain*, *hassle*, or *too much*; and when questioned will often reply, "I don't know." While interacting with this person, I am likely to feel frustrated or annoyed. The person with a self-control priority will likely maintain an impassive facial expression and little body movement and will make sparse or measured use of unemotional words; while interacting with this person, I am likely to feel distanced emotionally. The person with a control-of-others priority will likely make challenging eye contact; use negative and imperative words such as *should*; and be angry, blaming, and critical. While interacting with this person, I am likely to feel challenged to an actual or potential power struggle.

Using Personality Priorities in Counseling

From the time I first meet a client couple, I begin to observe their actions and words and my own emotional responses to them. On this basis, usually during the first session, and not later than the end of the second session, I have formulated a hypothesis about each client's priority. If the priority phenomenon seems to be related to the clients' distress and their expressed issues and goals in counseling, I proceed with the following steps.

I introduce the concept of personality priorities to the clients:

> In my work with people, I've found that different people have different priorities in life—what I call *personality priorities*. Everyone's is unique, but I've found there are five broad categories. Most people identify with at least one of these categories. Each priority has its benefits and drawbacks. Although the names of the priorities, like *control* and *pleasing*, may have negative or positive connotations, in fact no one priority is better than another; they each have their advantages and disadvantages. Knowing my priority has been helpful to me. I have a hunch that knowing yours might help you with the issues you came to counseling to resolve. I'd like to describe the priorities; as I do, be putting them in a rank order from "most like me" to "least like me" and simultaneously "most like my partner" to "least like my partner." How does this sound to you?

I have never had a client refuse, but if one did, I would drop the subject. Ideally, at least one of the clients would bring up the subject at a later time. If not, and if I continued to believe that the exploration of priorities would be therapeutically beneficial, I would watch for a promising time to reopen the topic. At the point they agreed, I would continue:

> I'd like to go through all five descriptions without discussion. If you don't understand something, of course, let me know, and I'll do my best to clarify. Otherwise, just listen and do the prioritizing in your head regarding both yourself and your partner.

I would then present the priorities in a particular order that pertains specifically to the couple I am seeing. Whichever priorities I had hypothesized to be the clients' I present last. If I were to present their priorities first, they likely would listen less attentively to the remaining ones. By presenting their priorities last, I maximize the likelihood they will remain attentive throughout the explanation.

As I present the priorities, I am careful to be objective in my description so I do not betray which priorities I have hypothesized to be the clients'. I also watch the clients' nonverbal reactions. They often respond to the description of their own or their partner's priority with "recognition reflexes." On hearing their own, clients often smile slightly and briefly break eye contact with me—although a client with one of the control priorities would be less likely to reveal recognition of his or her priority. On hearing the partner's priority, a client will often look knowingly at the partner. I do not respond to these nonverbal messages; I merely make a mental note of them and continue with my objective description:

> One priority is pleasing. A pleasing person seeks to please others even at his or her own expense or detriment. Advantages are that the pleaser is cooperative and is sensitive and responsive to the needs and wishes of others. Disadvantages include sometimes not knowing one's own wants or feeling stressed if too many people want mutually exclusive things. The pleaser seeks acceptance; the condition most avoided is rejection.
>
> Another priority is superiority. The superiority person seeks to be right, competent, the best. Some advantages are that the superiority person is often organized, focused, and accomplishes a great deal. Disadvantages are that the person may be perceived as a workaholic who doesn't relax and who neglects personal relationships. The superiority person seeks meaningfulness, to make a significant contribution; the condition most avoided is meaninglessness.
>
> A third priority is comfort. Someone with a comfort priority tries to enjoy pleasures without having to wait or having to exert oneself. Some advantages are that the comfort person is relaxed, easygoing, spontaneous, often charming, and not likely to suffer from stress-related problems. Some disadvantages include not accomplishing a great deal and being less reliable than others might be. The comfort person seeks to be stress free; the condition most avoided is stress in any form.
>
> Another priority is self-control. The self-control person seeks to manage what is inside him- or herself, to keep feelings under control by being very reserved and composed. Some advantages are that this person is stable, reliable, and practical. Disadvantages include emotional distance and diminished spontaneity and creativity. The self-control person seeks to hide inner processes from others; the condition most avoided is the vulnerability of one's inner workings showing, particularly one's emotions.
>
> A final priority is control of others. The person with this priority seeks to manage what is outside him- or herself, including situations and people. Some advantages include an ability to take charge and make things happen. Some disadvantages include that others tend to withdraw or attack in response to a control-of-others person. This person seeks to be in charge; the condition to be most avoided is the vulnerability of feeling out of control of one's surroundings.

When I have finished the descriptions, I ask the clients to identify their own and their partner's first priority. If a client cannot decide between two or more priorities, I ask the client to think of a situation in which the priorities were in conflict and then to recall which priority "won out" over the other; the winning priority is probably the number one priority. To clarify, I sometimes use myself as an example. My top two priorities are superiority and pleasing. My husband once invited me to write a book with him. I asked what he and I had to say on the subject that had not already been said. He replied that we would not necessarily say anything new, but we would say it in a new way. He emphasized that he would really like for us to undertake this project together. My superiority resisted doing such a "meaningless" activity that would not make a significant contribution to the professional literature, although my pleasing resisted displeasing him and risking his rejection. The fact that I declined to write the book with him suggests that superiority is my first personality priority.

When the couple indicate that they have come to a preliminary conclusion about their own and their partner's first priorities, I invite either to begin and the partner to follow in stating his or her hypotheses. If the clients agree with each other and with me about each of their priorities (as, in my clinical experience, we almost always do), I do not say, "Right." By implying they were correct, I would attribute to myself more expertise than I believe is warranted. Instead I say, "That was my guess, too." I then encourage each member of the couple to explain how he or she came to that conclusion. When they finish, I begin by reiterating points they made with which I agree, then I continue to add any additional points that they did not mention. At this point, I may bring in references to their nonverbal and verbal behaviors that coincide with their respective hypothesized personality priorities.

If clients identify different priorities than I would hypothesize, I listen, reflect back to them what they are asserting, and pursue how they came to their conclusions. If their thinking seems to have been based on a misunderstanding of the information, I offer correct information. If they persist in a conclusion different from mine, I acknowledge their perspective and say that I had come to a different conclusion. I explain the basis of my conclusion. If they continue to disagree, I say something like, "Even though we don't see your priorities the same way, I am glad we explored this subject." I avoid getting into power struggles with clients over who is right and who is wrong. At some later point, the clients and I may come to see eye to eye, at which point we pursue the topic.

At the point that we agree on the clients' personality priorities, I explain how the interaction of their priorities relates to their counseling goals. For example, the interaction of the couple's priorities has implications for conflict reduction, usually one of the clients' counseling goals. A superiority person who has difficulty relaxing may be coupled with a comfort person who is an expert on relaxation; the comfort person who accomplishes very little is in relationship with a superiority person who accomplishes a great deal. Similarly, someone whose priority is to control others may be coupled with someone whose priority is to please. In both types of couples, the complementarity may have provided a basis for attraction, but over time the oppositional aspects of complementarity emerge. The superiority seeker wants the comfort seeker to get up and accomplish something, but that would mean the comfort seeker undertaking stress, his or her condition to be most avoided. Conversely, the comfort seeker wants the superiority seeker to come relax with him or her, but that would mean the superiority seeker engaging in meaninglessness activity, his or her condition to be most avoided. Similarly, one who seeks to control a pleasing partner never allows him or herself to be pleased. To do so would mean giving up control of the partner; the pleaser cannot please, is frustrated, and begins to be less cooperative, creating for the controller the condition to be most avoided: loss of control. In each of these pairings, the partners perceive themselves to be in existential crisis and are likely in conflict.

In my clinical experience, the most common pairings to present in couples counseling are superiority–comfort and control of others–pleasing. Main and Oliver (1988) found the lowest self-reported marital adjustment among just such "complementary" couples, who constituted 64% of the couples whose data was useable. They found that the minority of couples who match priorities were significantly better maritally adjusted, which matches my clinical observation that such couples rarely present for couples counseling (Holden, 1991).

To ease a couple's sense of crisis and reduce conflict, the therapeutic goal is not to change anyone's priority but rather to reduce the extremity with which each partner expresses his or her priority. According to the concept of "extremity of expression," the moderately strong expression of a priority maximizes the advantages of the priority, whereas extreme expression exacerbates the disadvantages. By reducing the extremity of expression of their respective priorities, detrimental aspects are reduced, beneficial aspects are enhanced, and both the sense of crisis and the feeling and expression of conflict are minimized.

Specifically, the couple comes to understand each partner's priority, including characteristics, purpose, and condition to be most avoided, as well as the complementary nature of their attraction to each other and the oppositional aspects that have emerged from that complementarity. Then each is helped to see how a modification of the expression of the priority might be realized. The comfort seeker is encouraged to make the effort to tackle stress (such as taking out the garbage) more frequently (but not always) rather than avoiding it. The superiority seeker learns to say no occasionally to the new project at work that will result in exhaustion and neglect of family. The control-of-others person develops positive interaction patterns that communicate satisfaction, such as reducing criticism and enhancing the expression of gratitude and positive evaluation. The pleaser is encouraged to develop an awareness of personal preferences and appropriate personal boundaries. The self-controller is helped to become more aware and expressive of feelings, playfulness, and creativity.

As partners become less polarized in the oppositional aspects of their complementary priorities, their intrapersonal sense of crisis and interpersonal pattern of conflict reduce. In addition, each can be encouraged to empathize with the partner's personality priority. They learn that their partner's priority comes from an early conclusion that the enactment of the priority seemed to be the best way to maximize pleasure and minimize pain in life. They also learn how they were attracted to aspects of the partner's priority that represent deficits in their own priority. In addition, they are helped to acknowledge that it is just as difficult for the partner to achieve personality priority modification as it is for oneself. Thus, a partner's occasional reversions to earlier patterns, if not excessive, are probably best tolerated, and the partner's successes in modification are definitely best met with acknowledgment and appreciation.

A brief comment about the control-of-others priority is warranted. In my clinical experience, clients with this priority have been least willing to acknowledge their priority—probably because to admit one's strategy as controlling is to relinquish control. I have sometimes succeeded in achieving a client's acknowledgment of his or her control-of-others priority, especially with the assistance of the spouse, but I often have not. In these cases, rather than risk destroying a therapeutic alliance, I back off from the subject and refer back to it only on rare and well-timed occasions. To date, my best response to this situation is acceptance of possible limitations in impacting the couple therapeutically as long as the controller is unwilling to acknowledge the priority.

Conclusion

Addressing personality priorities is an intervention I have found useful in helping couples understand and modify a source of their distress and conflict. Clients have mostly evaluated this component of their counseling as anywhere from moderately to extremely helpful. Once introduced to the therapeutic material, clients—and I—frequently refer to it throughout their couples counseling.

References

Brown, J. F. (1976). *Practical application of the personality priorities: A guide for counselors* (2nd ed.). Clinton, MD: B&F Associates.

Holden, J. M. (1991). The most frequent personality priority pairings in marriage and marriage counseling. *Individual Psychology, 47,* 392–398.

Langenfeld, S., & Main, F. (1983). Personality priorities: A factor analytic study. *Individual Psychology, 39,* 40–51.

Main, F., & Oliver, R. (1988). Complementary, symmetrical, and parallel personality priorities as indicators of marital adjustment. *Individual Psychology, 44,* 324–332.

■ ■ ■

5

Using Play Therapy to Assess Family Dynamics

Daniel S. Sweeney, PhD
Sharon L. Rocha, MA

Many therapists working with families exclude children, particularly young children, from participation in family therapy sessions (Chasin, 1989; Gil, 1994). In our work with families, however, we have found that the inclusion of children greatly enriches the therapeutic process. Whole-family sessions not only enhance the therapeutic understanding of both the child and the family, they also reinforce the systemic orientation by including all of the family members present in the current family system. Having the entire family present in family therapy provides a more accurate picture of family dynamics, as members continue to play the same roles that they play in their home situation.

The inclusion of children in family therapy provides the clinician the opportunity to observe patterns of communication, roles, coalitions, and triangles rather than working from assumptions based on the self-report of a few individuals. This gives the clinician the opportunity to view the complexity of interactions within the family gestalt and to observe how family dynamics are affected by individual development and family life-cycle needs. We believe, therefore, that if the whole family is to be treated therapeutically, the whole family should be included in the assessment and treatment process.

Assessment and treatment of families with young children must include an orientation and techniques that include and honor the world of children. We believe that this is the world of play. Involving children in family therapy through the world of play and play therapy is not only effective but also truly inclusive, which should be the goal of any systemic-oriented therapist.

Children in Family Therapy

A variety of schools of family therapy, including strategic, systemic, experiential, and behavioral, have traditions that encourage active engagement of children (Chasin, 1989). Family sculpting (Papp, Silverstein, & Carter, 1973)—in which the physical arrangement of the family system is determined by an individual member as a director—and structural therapy's enactment (Minuchin, 1974)—in which a family is asked, during a therapy session, to spontaneously act out new ways of relating—are examples of such engagement. The efficacy of such techniques with children, however, is not clear, although we might suggest they may require abstract thinking and practical assertiveness that many children find challenging.

We would assert that the family therapist wanting to actively engage children must be intentional about the process. Korner and Brown (1990), in their study of family therapists who either included or excluded children from the family therapy process, found that family therapists who had received specialized training with children or who felt that their training with children was adequate were more likely to include children in the therapy process.

In addition, it is our observation of the family therapy world that inclusion of children has not been the priority it should be. Although some have focused on the involvement of children in family therapy, on review, a great number of articles and books in the field of family therapy do not include the words *children* or *play* in their indexes. At best, the practice simply seems to be somewhat inconsistent. Chasin and White (1989) agreed with this, asserting that "in actual practice, children are more frequently excluded than included in family therapy" (p. 5).

In spite of this lack, however, the importance of including children in the family therapy process has not been entirely unrecognized by those in the field. Nathan Ackerman (1970), one of the pioneers in the field, wrote that "without engaging the children in a meaningful interchange across the generations, there can be no family therapy" (p. 403). The question, therefore, involves how this might be done. Following his above assertion, Ackerman (1970) went on to suggest that "in the daily practice of this form of treatment, difficulties in mobilizing the participation of children are a common experience" (p. 403). If family therapy is going to be truly systemic, all members of the family must be recognized as making a contribution.

As integral components of the family unit, children often provide access to family problems by making the problem visible to others (Zilbach, 1986). This aids early detection of potential problem areas as well as potential family strengths. In working with children and their families, we have found that the inclusion of children in the therapeutic process is essential to understanding the family's past development as well as current structure and patterns of communication.

Play Therapy

Before discussing specific family play therapy techniques, it seems important to briefly discuss the world of play therapy. Landreth (1991) defined play therapy as a "dynamic interpersonal relationship between a child and a therapist trained in play therapy procedures who provides selected play materials and facilitates the development of a safe relationship for the child to fully express and explore self (feelings, thoughts, experiences, and behaviors) through the child's natural medium of communication, play" (p. 14).

It is essential for therapists to realize that play is the most important and most natural activity of childhood and it is the way children process and express their emotional life. The counselor who understands the importance of play to children is well on the way to understanding them. For children, play is as natural and spontaneous as any other daily activity. They not only play for the sake of play, they also play to make sense of their world. For the child in a family experiencing conflict or crisis, this can be crucial. Landreth (1991) asserted that, "for children to 'play out' their experiences and feelings is the most natural dynamic and self-healing process in which children can engage" (p. 10). This is a critical understanding. When we recognize that children's play is their natural medium of communication, it should become evident that therapy involving children must include play.

Family Play Therapy

We would like to make two points at the outset of this discussion. First, we suggest that the marriage of family therapy and play therapy is a natural union. Eliana Gil (1994) posited that family therapists and play therapists share a noble trait: They are by far the most creative and dynamic therapists in existence. Family therapists . . . engage the family's participation in a dynamic way, either by intensifying or replacing verbal communication" (p. 34). These qualities can and should be harnessed to include even very young children in the family therapy process. Second, we would encourage the interested reader to seek out appropriate and adequate training in play therapy.

What is family play therapy? Eaker (1986) remarked that family play therapy combines play techniques with family systems therapy and offers the benefits of each" (p. 236). Keith and Whitaker (1981) included play therapy as an integral part of the family treatment process, concluding that "fundamental family therapy takes place at this nonverbal level" (p. 249). It is our belief that family play therapy is a truly inclusive intervention for the presenting family with young children, providing both the therapist and other family members with a more complete picture of family dynamics and processes.

Family therapy must address the "lowest developmental denominator." This means the children. Few of us would deny the contribution that children make to the function or dysfunction of a family system. Acknowledging this contribution and including children in the therapy process, in a manner that is developmentally appropriate and equitable, however, is not so easy. Keith and Whitaker (1981) shared this concern: "Modern child psychiatry worries about children in family therapy being overlooked and excluded . . . It is important to include children because of their developmental needs. On the other hand, families need the presence of children in therapy to stay alive. We find again and again that families change less and more slowly when children are not part of the therapy process" (p. 244).

The inclusion of children in family therapy requires therapists to be aware of children's special developmental needs. Developmentally, children lack the ability for introspection and cannot deal with feelings at an adult level (Logan, 1987). Although some children, particularly those of latency age, may seem to relate verbally, verbal interchange is an insufficient mode of expression for their feelings and thoughts. The use of play provides a mode for working with these different developmental needs. It provides the concrete mode of expression appropriate to children's developmental needs, thus removing the practice barrier for the active participation of children in family therapy and providing a mode of communication that levels the playing field among individuals at different levels of cognitive and affective development.

Remember that the preoperational and concrete nature of children's cognitive and affective life is generally incompatible with the formal operations of "adult" family therapy. Children under the age of 12 years typically do not have the mastery of language and abstract thinking necessary to process and verbalize like adults. The developmental sophistication necessary for the abstract reasoning on which most verbal therapies are built is simply beyond most children. The family therapist must, therefore, make provision for children in the therapeutic process by honoring the preoperational world of childhood, the world of play.

In addition to leveling the playing field among the developmental levels of family members, play serves as a bridge between the constructed reality of the family and the ability of the therapist to appreciate that reality (Riley & Malchiodi, 1994). The content of the play provides a metaphorical blueprint of family alliances, intergenerational patterns, and stages of personality development. This largely undefended mode of expression provides the therapist with the opportunity to access information that may not be disclosed through verbal expression, as well as to observe the emotional climate of the family (Kwiatkowska, 1978). In addition, it allows for the expression of emotions that may be too difficult to express in words (Riley & Malchiodi, 1994).

It is not possible for us to launch into a full description of play therapy with families. As we describe a few techniques, it is important to note that we do not see the family therapy or play therapy process as prescriptive. Each person and each family has unique qualities and characteristics. Application of techniques, therefore, varies with every client and every family. Having said this, we have found the techniques described below as incredibly beneficial in the assessment and treatment of families with children.

Family Art Assessment

In working with families, art provides an alternative to verbal therapy in both assessment and treatment. Family art assessment is appropriate for use with individuals from approximately 4 years of age through adult (Logan, 1987). It is an activity that involves all family members simultaneously; minimizes the developmental differences in communication ability; records the structure, dynamics, and processes at work in the family system; and provides a concrete record for the ongoing assessment of change over the treatment period (Greenspoon, 1986). Although the content of the artwork may provide clues to the family system, the focus is primarily on process (Landgarten, 1987).

Our approach to family evaluations is rooted in family systems theory; thus, the emphasis of our evaluation is on the whole family rather than an "identified patient." For the purposes of our assessment, we have chosen to use the format for family evaluation developed by Landgarten (1987). This evaluation involves a series of three art tasks: (a) a nonverbal team task, (b) a nonverbal family art task, and (c) a verbal family art task. The materials required for the assessment include a table or other smooth surface large enough to seat all family members comfortably, enough colored markers for each member to choose a different color, and several sheets of drawing paper with a minimum size of 12 x 18in. (30 x 46cm). We have found that the assessment requires 1.5 to 2 hours to complete.

Procedure

Once the therapist has introduced him- or herself to the family and addressed the reason the family members were all asked to attend, the therapist might introduce the art assessment in the following manner: "In working with families, family therapists often use a variety of techniques to learn more about the family. We began by talking to each other, but we could also use acting, puppetry, or play. Today we're going to use art to learn more about each other."

If concerns are raised at this point about the validity of art as an assessment tool, we merely assure the family that the art exercise is a standardized tool for assessing how the family functions as a group. Family members who raise concerns about their level of artistic ability can be reassured by stating that how well they draw is not a concern. The primary message here is one of uncritical acceptance of each family member, as well as his or her artwork.

The first task, the nonverbal team art task, begins when the family is asked to divide into two teams. The composition of the teams provides information on family alliances, and issues of control and power are illustrated by the way the two teams are formed. Each team is given its own sheet of paper. In introducing the first task, the therapist might use the following directive: "The first task we're going to do requires you to divide up into two teams. You can choose the teams any way you want, then let me know when you have decided (pause). All right, now I'd like each of you to choose a different colored marker. You can only choose one marker, and you will use that marker for the whole session (pause). Now, when I tell you to begin, each team is to begin working on their piece of paper. There is one special rule; you may not talk, signal, or write notes to each other while you're working on the artwork, and when you're done, you should just stop. Are there any questions?"

If the teams have not completed their work after 20 minutes, the therapist informs them that their time is up and that they are to stop. The teams are then instructed to decide on a title for their artwork and to write it on the work. Talking is permitted for this task. Note that no specific directives have been given to the family in regard to the content of the artwork. Occasionally, however, we will give directed art activities, such as the Kinetic Family Drawing (Burns & Kaufman, 1980).

The next task is the nonverbal family art task. The following directive may be used to introduce this task: "In this exercise the whole family will work together on the same sheet of paper. Use the same marker that you used for the last project, and just like the first time, no talking, signaling, or writing notes."

As with the first task, if the family has not completed their artwork after 20 minutes, the therapist should inform them that their time is up and that they are to stop. The family is then instructed to decide on a title and to write it on the artwork.

The third and final task, the verbal family art task, may be introduced in the following manner: "For our last drawing, the whole family will again work together on one sheet of paper. This time, however, talking is permitted."

When the family is finished the task, they are instructed to decide on a title and write it on the artwork.

Much of the assessment information that can be gleaned from the session is obtained by the therapist's recording of his or her observations during the session. The following list of questions, based on Landgarten (1987), may be used to guide this process:

1. What was the process that led to the formation of the two teams? Who initiated the process, and what were the interactions that followed?
2. Who began each art task, and what was the process that led up to the initiation? What was the order of the other family

members' participation? Was there a shift in approach at any point? If so, who initiated the change?

3. Did the family members work simultaneously, in teams, or by taking alternate turns? What was the level of involvement of each family member? How much space did each member use? What were the geographical locations of each member's contribution? What was the symbolic content of each person's contribution?

4. Was the family members' working style cooperative, discordant, or individualistic? Which family member acted as an initiator, a follower, or a reactor? Which family member(s) functioned independently? Which family member's suggestions were used and which were ignored?

5. Which family members remained in their own space, and which crossed over? Did anyone negate another family member's contribution by superimposing his or her image over someone else's? Were emotional responses made?

Family Puppet Evaluation

As noted previously, it can be very threatening to ask a child to detail the communication patterns in the family through words. It can be equally threatening for any member of the family who feels isolated or disempowered. Put simply, it is not okay to "air the dirty laundry," especially to an outsider. Children should not talk about problems, but perhaps puppets can! The therapeutic and assessment value of puppets was noted by Bow (1993), who stated that puppet play "creates an unrealistic and nonthreatening atmosphere that assists in the identification process, thereby encouraging the projection of emotional aspects and interpersonal relationships through the characters" (p. 28).

The use of puppets as a therapeutic technique with children is not a new phenomenon. Using puppets as an assessment tool has been described by Irwin and Shapiro (1975), Webb (1991), Bow (1993), and others. As a therapeutic technique, puppets represent another projective medium through which children can process their issues. Irwin and Malloy (1975) described the "family puppet interview," which provides the basis for our suggested intervention.

There are numerous ways in which to structure a family puppet interview. Some therapists who use puppets will direct the parents or the children to act out a particular scene from the family's life. This can be a helpful tool. In terms of initial family assessment, however, such direct instructions may be too threatening to some family members. We prefer to simply request that the family perform a simple puppet play, creating whatever story they wish. This gives the therapist the opportunity to assess family dynamics.

The following materials are suggested. We prefer to have a puppet theater of some sort to optimally facilitate the "performance" of the puppet play. A simple wooden structure that is hinged and folds flat for easy storage is best. It is important that the stage window of this puppet theater be low enough for young children to reach. If such a puppet theater is not possible, having a family perform the puppet play behind a piece of office furniture will work as well.

A wide variety of puppets is crucial. There should be enough puppets so that each member of even a large family can select two or three puppets. A few comments are necessary regarding the puppets themselves. It is important that the puppets be gender and ethnically diverse; besides the need to provide a variety which will suit the diversity of families seeking treatment, it is important that the therapist demonstrate a sensitivity to diverse populations. Some puppet therapists would also recommend having puppets from varying occupational backgrounds. Additionally, we would recommend that a large number of the puppets be animals of various types.

Animal puppets are easy to obtain, or to make, and generally can be used without regard to gender and ethnicity. More significantly, however, animal puppets can represent family members in a protected and therapeutically distant manner. It is easier for family members, both young and old, to depict family interactions using animal puppets because a raccoon representing Dad is safer than an adult male puppet. It might be more okay to "act out" family crises or communication difficulties through animal puppets, as opposed to human puppets, and it is certainly easier than cognitive verbalization.

Procedure

The structure of using puppets as an assessment tool when working with families may vary. Generally, we begin by explaining what we would like to do with the family. It is not unusual to have one or more family member balk at such a "frivolous" play activity, but the dynamics of the family group process (especially the normal enthusiasm of the children) will normally persuade reluctant individuals. The need to be included and feel some sense of control will motivate most adult family members.

The process involves each family member selecting several puppets from the collection, which should be spread out before the family on a shelf or on the floor. It is our experience that many family members, especially young children, will not rummage through a container of puppets, such as a box or basket. Because they will usually select from the top of the container, it is better to spread them out. Prior to the performance, it is often helpful to have the family members talk about the puppets they have selected. We hesitate in asking why the family members selected a particular puppet because such questions require cognitive and abstract thinking processes that are beyond the ability of young children.

The puppet play may be planned by the family, but it may become necessary for the therapist to encourage the family to begin the puppet play, as some will keep the process too cognitive and less spontaneous. Nevertheless, family members, rather than the therapist, should dictate the process of the play. As the performance unfolds, typical family communication patterns and dysfunctional processes become evident. The verbally astute family member who rationalizes during therapeutic discussion and the withdrawn or apathetic family member will not be able to obscure important issues.

It is not necessary to be precise about the length of the puppet performance, except in terms of session length. There does need to be adequate time to verbally process the "drama," and the metaphorical and concrete material that the therapist usually has at this point is remarkable. There is often enough material discovered for sessions to come. Two warnings are offered at this point. First, the therapist is cautioned against using the abundant material that often develops through this projective technique to map out a therapeutic course that does not include children in the treatment process. Second, the therapist is cautioned against being too interpretive because the most important interpretations in therapy are those of the clients.

Some questions to consider during and after the puppet performance are these:

1. Who initiated the choreography and direction of the play? Did anyone dominate?
2. Did the family (puppets) work together? Were any family members ignored in the process?
3. What was the level of dependence or independence of each puppet?

4. Did any puppet isolate him- or herself?
5. Who contributed least? Most?
6. Was the process smooth? Rigid? Chaotic?
7. How did the puppets communicate with each other? Did you see patterns, roles, coalitions, triangles?

The therapist may choose to "interview" the puppets in the play. This is best done by the therapist using a puppet and communicating with the other puppets, as opposed to directly asking anything of a family member. We suggest asking questions in the form of statements, which is always less threatening. For example, when exploring why one family member seemed to exclude him- or herself from the others, the therapist might say through her puppet, "I wonder why the beaver played a lot over here?" or "Looks like the beaver was pretty busy over here doing something by itself. Hmm." Questions like these offer opportunities for the beaver to respond but does not make it feel compelled to do so.

Puppets provide clients of any age a means to express issues and emotions that otherwise might be too challenging to address. The family experiencing dysfunction will often be able to express themselves through this projective means. The puppet play creates both a literal and metaphorical avenue for evaluation and intervention. The family therapist may enter this metaphorical realm, not only to increase clinical understanding but also to initiate therapeutic change.

Family Doll House Play

A doll house is considered a crucial tool for the play therapist. A child in treatment is provided the opportunity to play out scenes and issues from the home experience using dolls or animals. The safety that comes from the therapeutic distance of using dolls often enables a child to describe and process painful issues from his or her home life. Likewise, the doll house can be a wonderful tool for assessing the dynamics of a family within the family therapy process.

The use of sculpting as a family therapy technique (Papp et al., 1973) has traditionally involved providing each family member the opportunity to physically sculpt the family structure through the positioning of family members according to the individual's perspective. This may clearly provide a picture of the family dynamics for both the therapist and the family. The young child, however, is placed at an automatic disadvantage in this process. To ask a child to perform such a task is often overwhelming. When the child is able to perform the task, he or she may be focused on pleasing parents and adults, which can influence the sculpted structure.

Doll house play provides the sculpting opportunity in another manner. The therapist may simply introduce sculpting but ask the family members to use doll figures and the doll house instead of other family members. We suggest that the therapist using this technique begin with the children, so that their setup of the doll house will be less likely to be influenced by older family members. Most often, we simply ask family members to create a scene in the doll house using the doll figures.

Once again, the materials necessary for this assessment or intervention are simple but important. A doll house that is adequate in size is crucial. Some choose a two-story portable doll house, which is certainly adequate; we use a one-floor doll house that is completely open on the top. It is easier to move dolls and furniture and gives everyone in the room an opportunity to view the activity. It is important not to have materials that are too small and difficult to handle. Additionally, a doll house that is too fancy and colorful may be an obstacle for those clients from lower socioeconomic backgrounds. The rule of thumb is to have a simple and durable structure.

The furniture should also be simple and durable (we use wood) and should offer a broad reflection of an average house. Therefore, kitchen, bathroom, and bedroom furniture is essential. Living room and dining room furniture is also important. Additional doll furnishings may also be added. Again, it is best not to get too elaborate.

Like the puppets discussed above, it is important that the dolls demonstrate ethnic and gender diversity. A Caucasian family of four will hardly be useful for the Hispanic family of seven. The therapist should consider the ethnocultural background of his or her clients, as well as the local community. Animal families may also be helpful. We do not presuppose any family's preferences for dolls during this procedure; all family members may select their own. The preadolescent who feels disempowered may want to select the largest (or smallest) doll to represent internal and relational issues.

Procedure

Similar to puppet play, the structured use of the doll house as an assessment tool for families will vary. It is always important to begin by explaining the purpose and process of the intervention with the family. Again, one or more of the family members may balk at the "frivolous" or "childish" nature of the activity. As noted, this is generally not a significant concern. Additionally, it may be a significant teaching opportunity. If one or more family members raise an objection, it is likely that there are other concerns to address. Could it be that the father who objects to this play during the therapy process is one who is uninvolved and distant in out-of-session family matters? Does the reluctance reflect a lack of commitment to the therapeutic process? If any members of the family are not committed to counseling beyond a simple verbal assent, any expressive or projective intervention may be threatening. The therapist may use this reluctance or refusal as an opportunity to explore personal commitment and therapeutic goals.

There are two primary ways in which we use the doll house with families. The first is to use the doll house and dolls as a miniature sculpting exercise. Instead of asking each family member to arrange persons and furniture in the therapy room to illustrate family structure and dynamics, which can be fairly overwhelming for young children, we ask that the same be done in the doll house with doll figures. The same evaluatory material gained from traditional sculpting can be obtained with the doll house.

Some therapists note that in their experience, sculpting has not been an overwhelming experience for children. The simplicity and honesty of childhood may well elicit significant information from a traditional sculpting exercise. However, our concern would be that because most children inherently wish to please adults, other family members will potentially influence their sculpting. The doll house, however, represents the child's playground, where he or she is most likely to give an accurate and honest depiction of family life.

The other way we use the doll house is similar to the Kinetic Family Drawing (Burns & Kaufman, 1980), in which we simply ask each family member to create a scene in the doll house of the family doing something. This can be done with each individual family member or with the family as a whole, creating a similar dynamic to the puppet play. The specific direction to have the family (dolls) doing something helps to ensure that each family member will create a scene of the typical family functioning from his or her own perspective.

Conclusion

Family play therapy is a relatively new term in the counseling world. It is the natural marriage of two fields that extensively complement each other. We cannot underscore enough the value of using play therapy within the family therapy process. We discussed only

three of many possible family play therapy techniques. Family therapists have long professed an interest and priority in treating all
members of the family equally. When play is introduced into family
therapy, the process becomes comprehensive and inclusive. Play
"levels the playing field" for all the players. We encourage the reader:
Get the training, honor children, honor families. They will thank
you for it.

References

Ackerman, N. W. (1970). Child participation in family therapy. *Family Process, 9*, 403–410.

Bow, J. N. (1993). Overcoming resistance. In C. Schaefer (Ed.), *The therapeutic powers of play* (pp. 17–40). Northvale, NJ: Jason Aronson.

Burns, R. C., & Kaufman, S. (1980). *Kinetic Family Drawings* (K-F-D). New York: Brunner/Mazel.

Chasin, R. (1989). Interviewing families with children: Guidelines and suggestions. *Journal of Psychotherapy and the Family, 5*, 15–30.

Chasin, R., & White, T. (1989). The child in family therapy: Guidelines for active engagement across the life span. In L. Combrinck-Graham (Ed.), *Children in family contexts: Perspectives on treatment* (pp. 5–25). New York: Guilford Press.

Eaker, B. (1986). Unlocking the family secret in family play therapy. *Child and Adolescent Social Work, 3*, 235–253.

Gil, E. (1994). *Play in family therapy.* New York: Guilford Press.

Greenspoon, D. B. (1986). Multiple-family group art therapy. *Art Therapy, 3*, 53–60.

Irwin, E. C., & Malloy, E. S. (1975). Family puppet interview. *Family Process, 14*, 170–191.

Irwin, E. C., & Shapiro, M. (1975). Puppetry as a diagnostic and therapeutic technique. In I. Jakab (Ed.), *Psychiatry and art (Vol. 4).* Baseal, Switzerland: Karger.

Keith, D. V., & Whitaker, C. A. (1981). Play therapy: A paradigm for working with families. *Journal of Marital and Family Therapy, 7*, 243–254.

Korner, S., & Brown, G. (1990). Exclusion of children from family psychotherapy: Family therapists' beliefs and practices. *Journal of Family Psychology, 3*, 420-430.

Kwiatkowska, H. (1978). *Family therapy and evaluation through art.* Springfield, IL: Charles C. Thomas.

Landgarten, H. (1987). *Family art psychotherapy.* New York: Brunner/Mazel.

Landreth, G. L. (1991). *Play therapy: The art of the relationship.* Muncie, IN: Accelerated Development.

Logan, S. L. (1987). Practice considerations for working with children in family treatment. *Arete, 12*, 21–30.

Minuchin, S. (1974). *Families and family therapy*. Cambridge, MA: Harvard University Press.

Papp, P., Silverstein, O., & Carter, E. (1973). Family sculpting in preventive work with well families. *Family Process, 12*, 197–212.

Riley, S., & Malchiodi, C. A. (1994). *Integrative approaches to family art therapy*. Chicago: Magnolia Street.

Webb, N. B. (Ed.). (1991). *Play therapy with children in crisis*. New York: Guilford Press.

Zilbach, J. J. (1986). *Young children in family therapy*. New York: Brunner/ Mazel.

■ ■ ■

6

Graphic Perceptions

Frank M. Dattilio, PhD

M arital and family therapists will probably agree that one of the finest tools they can have during the course of treatment is the use of creative visual techniques for the expression of feelings and emotions. The professional literature is replete with various descriptions of games and activities as well as written exercises that couples and family therapists use in a creative fashion to promote change. These techniques are a fine method to be used in conducting an assessment as well as reducing the monotony that accompanies listening to complaints from couples in distress.

One technique that I use in the course of an assessment with couples is an exercise using paper, pencil, and circles drawn by each spouse to represent his or her perceptions and expectations of the relationship as well as hope for relationship improvement.

This exercise, similar to one first introduced by Weeks and Treat (1992), involves providing both spouses with a two-sided, blank piece of paper and a pencil and asking them to draw two circles, one to represent themselves and the other their partner. This is designed to indicate the proximity in which they view themselves within the relationship. The basic tenet is that the proximity of the circles rep-

The author acknowledges Francis S. Gaal, MEd, for providing the basic idea of using circles as a method of expression in couples therapy.

resents whether they view themselves as being emotionally close together or distant. Spouses will often draw circles that may be portrayed by Example A or Example B in Figure 6.1. Example A portrays the perception that some distance exists in the relationship, whereas B suggests more cohesiveness.

Both spouses should be sitting separately so that they cannot see each other's drawing. The next step is to ask them to turn the paper over and, using the same types of circles, indicate how they would like their relationship to be. Once again the proximity of the circles is used to represent either a closeness or a distance. Very commonly, therapists will see circles similar to those portrayed in Figure 6.2.

As can clearly be seen, Example A may be construed as an acceptable level of interaction, yet at the same time one that allows for independence or autonomy in the relationship. In Example B, the extreme exists, suggesting possible enmeshment or an unrealistic expectation, depending on what is presented and elaborated on by the other spouse.

The counselor suggests that couples swap papers and review each other's drawings. Discussion may ensue with regard to the differences in perception as well as realistic expectations. Partners are encouraged to share what each would like to see or expect the relationship to become and how viable this may be as a goal of therapy.

FIGURE 6.1

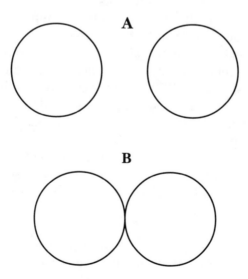

A

B

FIGURE 6.2

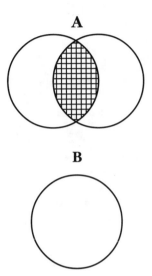

Conclusion

Using this technique provides the couple with a practical and visual means of helping them understand the differing perceptions that each spouse holds in their relationship. This activity may be repeated at intervals during the course of therapy and used to assess change as well as to provide some fun for the couple as they embark on the course of therapy.

References

Weeks, G. R., & Treat, S. (1992). *Couples in treatment: Techniques for effective practices*. New York: Brunner/Mazel.

■ ■ ■

7

Using the How I Remember My Family Questionnaire in Couples Counseling

Richard E. Watts, PhD

The How I Remember My Family Questionnaire (see Appendix A) was developed to assess the early recollections of couples regarding specific aspects of their families of origin. Alfred Adler and subsequent Adlerians have discussed the tremendous influence of the family on children as they creatively construct their lifestyle, the Adlerian nomenclature for personality. In addition, Adlerians have noted that one's early memories of family relations are equally important for how persons construe the roles and responsibilities of marital relations (Adler, 1956; 1979; Dinkmeyer, Dinkmeyer, & Sperry, 1987; Dreikurs, 1946; Manaster & Corsini, 1982; Mosak, 1984; Shulman & Watts, 1997; Sperry & Carlson, 1991).

The unique aspect of the questionnaire is that it helps in accessing aspects of Adlerian lifestyle information (see Baruth & Eckstein, 1981; Dinkmeyer et al., 1987; Eckstein, Baruth, & Mahrer, 1982; Mosak & Shulman, 1988) specifically relevant to premarital and marital

Portions of this chapter are taken from *The Family Journal, 3*, 155–157, 1995. © ACA. Used by permission.

counseling. Questions regarding the marital relationship of the individual's parents address selected key elements of marital relationships (Baruth & Huber, 1984; Dinkmeyer & Carlson, 1984, 1989; Dinkmeyer et al., 1987; Goldenberg & Goldenberg, 1996; Hawes & Kern, 1989; Ijams, 1989; Nichols, 1988). This seems a logical focus because a substantial body of literature suggests that the attitudes and actions of the marital/parent dyad in a system largely determines the family atmosphere, a crucial influence for the psychological development of children and their subsequent interpersonal relationships (e.g., Dewey, 1971; Dinkmeyer & McKay, 1996; Dinkmeyer, McKay, & Dinkmeyer, 1997; Dreikurs, 1946; Dreikurs & Soltz, 1964; Satir, 1983, 1988).

In premarital counseling, potential problem areas, if addressed at all, are often approached in terms of how the couple plans to negotiate them. In reality, most soon-to-be-married couples are oblivious to the impact of real or perceived family-of-origin issues and seldom are very objective regarding potential relationship difficulties. Likewise, in couples counseling, troubled couples seldom instinctively see how influential their perceptions of their family of origin may be for their current couple and family relationships. In both premarital and couples counseling, the questionnaire may be helpful in understanding both the clients as individuals and their couple relationship better and, consequently, may be useful in helping them become more aware of their relationship's assets and potential and current liabilities. By using the questionnaire as a guide, a great amount of information may be accessed and investigated by helpers skilled in using ancillary techniques, such as clarification, guided discovery, and Socratic dialogue.

Procedure

Both partners are given a copy of the questionnaire prior to leaving the initial session. The counselor asks them to answer the questions, independent of their partner, on separate sheets of paper and bring their answers to the next counseling session. The counselor should stress that they answer the questions in an open, honest manner and request that they not discuss their answers until the next scheduled meeting.

At the next session, the counselor begins helping the couple debrief from the questionnaire in whatever format is most comfortable. One suggestion is to let the couple take turns, working through the questionnaire section by section. Throughout the process I ask them to discuss questions such as (a) What did you learn about yourself and about your partner from this section of the exercise? and (b) What areas of agreement and disagreement did you discover? Furthermore, I offer hunches gleaned from their questionnaires—in the form of hypothesis questioning—and guide the couple in a discussion or dialogue.

The questionnaire debriefing and discussion may take more than one session. It is recommended that couples not discuss the questionnaire outside of session until it is completed. On the basis of the debriefing and discussion times, couples and counselors typically have a wealth of information for future counseling sessions, goal setting, and remediation.

Conclusion

The How I Remember My Family Questionnaire helps counselors obtain the early recollections of couples regarding their families of orgin. The questionnaire typically helps counselors bypass current tensions and potential resistances in the couple and is often useful in helping counselors and clients better understand the couple's relationship and its assets and potential liabilities.

References

Adler, A. (1956). *The individual psychology of Alfred Adler*. In H. L. Ansbacher & R. R. Ansbacher (Eds.). New York: Basic Books.

Adler, A. (1979). *Superiority and social interest*. In H. L. Ansbacher & R. R. Ansbacher (Eds.). New York: Norton.

Baruth, L., & Eckstein, D. (1981). *Life style: Theory, practice, and research* (2nd ed.). Dubuque, IA: Kendall/Hunt.

Baruth, L. G., & Huber, C. H. (1984). *An introduction to marital theory and therapy*. Monterey, CA: Brooks/Cole.

Dewey, E. (1971). Family atmosphere. In A.G. Nikelly (Ed.), *Techniques for behavior change* (pp. 41–48). Springfield, IL: Charles C. Thomas.

Dinkmeyer, D., & Carlson, J. (1984). *Time for a better marriage*. Circle Pines, MN: American Guidance Service.

Dinkmeyer, D., & Carlson, J. (1989). *Taking time for love: How to stay happily married*. New York: Prentice Hall.

Dinkmeyer, D., Dinkmeyer, D., Jr., & Sperry, L. (1987). *Adlerian counseling and psychotherapy* (2nd ed.). Columbus, OH: Charles E. Merrill.

Dinkmeyer, D., & McKay, G. D. (1996). *Raising a responsible child* (Rev. ed.). New York: Fireside.

Dinkmeyer, D., McKay, G. D., & Dinkmeyer, D., Jr. (1997). *The parent's handbook: Systematic training for effective parenting.* Circle Pines, MN: American Guidance Service.

Dreikurs, R. (1946). *The challenge of marriage.* New York: Hawthorne.

Dreikurs, R., & Soltz, V. (1964). *Children: The challenge.* New York: Hawthorne.

Eckstein, D., Baruth, L., & Mahrer, D. (1982). *Life style: What it is and how to do it* (2nd ed.). Dubuque, IA: Kendall/Hunt.

Goldenberg, I., & Goldenberg, H. (1996). *Family therapy: An overview* (4th ed.). Pacific Grove, CA: Brooks/Cole.

Hawes, E. C., & Kern, R. M. (1989). The initial interview. In R. M. Kern, E. C. Hawes, & O. C. Christensen (Eds.), *Couples therapy: An Adlerian perspective* (pp. 57–56). Minneapolis, MN: Educational Media.

Ijams, M. N. (1989). The lifestyle of a relationship. In R. M. Kern, E. C. Hawes, & O. C. Christensen (Eds.), *Couples therapy: An Adlerian perspective* (pp. 57–76). Minneapolis, MN: Educational Media.

Manaster, G. J., & Corsini, R. J. (1982). *Individual psychology.* Itasca, IL: Peacock.

Mosak, H. H. (1984). Adlerian psychotherapy. In R. J. Corsini (Ed.), *Current psychotherapies* (3rd ed., pp. 56–108). Itasca, IL: Peacock.

Mosak, H. H., & Shulman, B. H. (1988). *Life style inventory.* Muncie, IN: Accelerated Development.

Nichols, M. P. (1988). *The power of the family.* New York: Fireside.

Satir, V. (1983). *Conjoint family therapy* (3rd ed.). Palo Alto, CA: Science & Behavior Books.

Satir, V. (1988). *The new peoplemaking.* Palo Alto, CA: Science & Behavior Books.

Shulman, B. H., & Watts, R. E. (1997). Adlerian and constructivist theories: An Adlerian perspective. *The Journal of Cognitive Psychotherapy, 11,* 181–193.

Sperry, L., & Carlson, J. (1991). *Marital therapy: Integrating theory and technique.* Denver, CO: Love.

■ ■ ■

8

Using the BASIS–A Inventory With Couples

Mary S. Wheeler, PhD

The BASIS–A Inventory (Wheeler, Kern, & Curlette, 1983) is a brief, self-scoring inventory that can be very helpful in working with couples in therapy. The BASIS–A is unique in that all of the questions relate to a person's perceptions of his or her childhood. It provides measures on five primary scales (Belonging–Social Interest, Going Along, Taking Charge, Wanting Recognition, and Being Cautious) and five subscales to supplement interpretation of the primary scales (Harshness, Entitlement, Liked by All, Striving for Perfection, and Softness). The BASIS–A provides a quick assessment of a couple's level of adjustment as a couple and gives a helpful overview of some of the differences that affect their relationship and how they respond to the life task of developing intimacy.

Intimacy

The *BASIS–A Inventory Interpretive Manual* (Kern, Wheeler, & Curlette, 1997) provides interpretive information on each of the BASIS–A scales in relation to the life tasks of work, social relationships, and intimacy. A person's BASIS–A profile can provide helpful information as to how he or she will relate in the area of intimacy. A description of each of the primary scales and a brief summary of its relation to the task of intimacy follows.

Belonging–Social Interest

This theme measures a person's sense of belonging in the world and feelings of confidence about him- or herself. In an intimate relationship, a high scorer would tend to relate effectively to the other person, expecting the relationship to be a cooperative venture in which both individuals are treated with respect and give mutual support to the other. Low scorers may have more difficulty establishing a sense of belonging in the relationship and may need more encouragement and support from their partner.

Going Along

Individuals who score high on Going Along tend to be more comfortable when they know what the rules are and what is expected of them. Individuals who score low tend to be rebellious and argumentative. Individuals who score high or low may have difficulty with conflict within the relationship—high scorers sacrificing their own needs to avoid a conflict and low scorers possibly creating an argument to get their needs met.

Taking Charge

This scale measures the extent to which a person likes to be in charge and take on leadership roles. In an intimate relationship, a high scorer may be more of the decision maker in the couple and may be accused by his or her partner as being too assertive or controlling. When both partners score high, they may become involved in power struggles over who is to be in charge.

Wanting Recognition

Individuals who score high on Wanting Recognition are interested in achieving and obtaining the approval of people they respect. In an intimate relationship, individuals can validate their partner's successes. Low scorers may have difficulty doing this because they have not received recognition in their childhood and have little experience in how to give it.

Being Cautious

This scale reflects a dysfunctional family of origin and a resulting hesitancy to trust in relationships. High scorers may be inclined to take their partner's suggestions too personally and question whether they can trust their partner to meet their needs.

Couple Adjustment

Research has suggested that the more similar the couple's profiles are, the better adjusted they are likely to be (Harrison, 1993; Logan, Kern, Curlette, & Trad, 1993). Using data from 420 married couples, Harrison found that wives who were the most similar to their husbands on their Life Style Personality Inventory (LSPI, a research version of the BASIS–A) themes scored the highest on marital satisfaction. Husbands who were "somewhat similar" to their wives were happiest. The most different couples were the unhappiest.

Logan et al. (1993) also found a positive relationship between similarity of scores on the LSPI and couple adjustment scores on the Dyadic Adjustment Scale (DAS), which is designed to measure the quality of adjustment in marriage and other dyads. Additionally, she found that couples with high scores on the scale similar to Belonging–Social Interest had higher couple adjustment scores on the DAS. The more different couples were on a scale similar to Going Along, the less adjusted they were likely to be. Finally, the more different couples were on a scale similar to Being Cautious, the less adjusted they were likely to be.

This information concerning the adjustment of a couple can be used to encourage those couples who are similar. It can be pointed out that they have motivations in common that give strength to their relationship. For couples who are different, it can be pointed out that these are areas in which they need to work especially hard to understand their differences and how they affect their relationship.

Individual Differences

Individuals tend to assume the other person in the relationship has the same goals they do. When the other person disagrees with them, they may be inclined to take it personally. Seeing the differences in their BASIS–A profiles and seeing the connection between the problems they are experiencing and their childhood origins can help give the couple a different perspective on their differences. For example, when one person in the couple is more interested in following rules than the other, the other can be helped to understand that this began in childhood and is not necessarily an attack on the partner's character because they disagree.

Differences on any of the BASIS–A scales or subscales can be a reason for difficulty in adjusting as a couple. For example, if one partner is high on Entitlement and the other is low on Entitlement, he or she may have difficulty in sharing on an equal basis within the relationship. The person scoring high will expect to get whatever he or she wants; the person scoring low will have expectations of never being treated as special or important. These dynamics will certainly have an affect on how the couple relate to each other.

Couples who differ on Wanting Recognition may find that they struggle with how to support each other. The person scoring high will expect the partner to give him or her recognition and praise when they do well and to value his or her need for recognition from others. The person scoring low will be unlikely to do this because he or she has received little praise or recognition as a child and does not see it as something that is important. Couples can be taught how to give each other encouragement and how to appreciate the other's accomplishments in a way that is meaningful to the partner.

Conclusion

The BASIS–A Inventory can provide helpful information concerning how an individual responds to the life task of achieving intimacy. It can give counselors an idea about the couple's adjustment and about how differences between the partners affect their relationship issues. The BASIS–A can be sent home with the couple or taken and scored in the office because it takes only about 30 minutes for the whole process. It can help couples see how their personalities relate to their childhoods and thus further acceptance of each other's differences.

Further information concerning the BASIS–A Inventory can be obtained from TRT Associates, Inc., 65 Eagle Ridge Drive, Highlands, North Carolina 28741, or from their Web site at www.mindspring.com/~trtbasis. Inquiries regarding research or purchasing the BASIS–A materials can be sent to info@trt-basis.com.

References

Harrison, M. G. (1993). *The relationship among Adlerian life-style themes, gender roles, cooperative negotiation, and marital satisfaction.* Unpublished doctoral dissertation, Georgia State University, Atlanta.

Kern, R. M., Wheeler, M. S., & Curlette, W. L. (1997). *BASIS–A Inventory interpretive manual: A psychological theory.* Highlands, NC: TRT Associates.

Logan, E., Kern, R., Curlette, W., & Trad, A. (1993). Couples adjustment, life-style similarity, and social interest. *Individual Psychology, 49,* 456–467.

Wheeler, M. S., Kern, R. M., & Curlette, W. L. (1983). *The BASIS–A Inventory.* Highlands, NC: TRT Associates.

■ ■ ■

9

Perception Pie

John Zarski, PhD
Patricia Parr, PhD

Constantine (1984), Reiss (1981), and Kantor and Lehr (1975) contributed an understanding of paradigmatic frames to the marriage and family field. From their research, these authors suggested that couples operate as if guided by relationship paradigms. These relationship paradigms are developed over time and become enduring beliefs or assumptions about the relationship in particular and of marriages in general. Every couple has unique relationship paradigms that evolve from their own experiences and worldview. The theoretical framework that makes a paradigmatic view so useful in marital therapy is that it promotes the idea that no one single model of a successful marriage exists but rather that each couple has an overarching frame that is unique to their own relationship. A paradigmatic perspective provides the therapist with a more open stance to identify appropriate treatment interventions based on the uniqueness of each couple and their relationship paradigm.

Kantor and Lehr (1975) were the first to identify three of the four basic types of family paradigms: closed, random, and open. Families operating from a closed paradigm value tradition, hierarchy, and order. At the opposite end of the continuum are those operating from random paradigms that are guided by independence taking precedence over interdependence. The open paradigmatic view represents a synthesis of features from the closed and random. These families are organized in an egalitarian manner, with a value for collaboration between subsystems and consensual decision making (Nugent & Constantine, 1988).

The synchronous paradigm is the fourth type (Constantine, 1986; Constantine & Israel, 1985). It presents a worldview of implicit agreement and harmony. Individual needs are hard to discern because they are so entwined and similar to the family needs. Although originally developed as a way to view families, a paradigmatic perspective is easily adapted to guide an understanding of couples systems (Nugent & Constantine, 1988).

All four paradigms can operate to produce successful, although very different, marriages. In addition, all four paradigmatic perspectives can bring unique and different worldviews to how couples function and manage different roles in their relationship.

From a systemic view, the behavior of the marital dyad is seen as interactionally governed by the feedback between individuals in the relationship, as it is affected by the environment, which includes such things as work, children, extended family, and social support systems (with individual, couple, and family involved). The marital dyad is viewed as a goal-directed system that endeavors to satisfy the needs of the individuals, the couple, the family, and the environment. One of the typical sources of marital distress is the failure of the system to adapt to individually assigned roles. This process can cause marital distress in the form of role overload. Differences of opinion, and the ensuing conflict that can result, is not only inevitable but in many instances also desirable. However, difficulties can arise when a couple holds such differing paradigms or perceptions of their marital reality that they get caught in unproductive repetitive patterns of blame and anger.

Busy schedules and multiple roles often consume couples in today's world. Blame, faultfinding, and eventually ingrained conflictual patterns are often the result of spouses trying to accomplish too many tasks with too little room for error or pleasure. Couples who complain of exhaustion, lack of enjoyment in their marital relationship, anger at each other for not doing their share, or expectations of the other to do too much have often lost the ability to focus on the whole because they get caught in focusing on the parts. "He's working too many hours," "She doesn't spend enough time with the children," "He's not keeping up with his household chores"—the litany goes on and on. This is typically the time that one of the spouses will say in behavior or words, "I've had enough. I'm tired of carrying the load of the marriage [or the family] on my shoulders." It is also typically the time couples show up at the marital therapist's door, one spouse with the other in tow to be fixed or changed.

Perception Pie Procedure

One intervention that can be used for these types of presenting complaints is the "perception pie." This marital relationship technique helps couples increase their awareness of their own and their partner's perception of time commitments in the marriage, as well as giving couples a new way of looking at the whole of their relationship rather than just the parts. This type of intervention is particularly helpful in clarifying relationship roles and expectations. Problems that couples bring into therapy are explored with particular attention paid to constructing reciprocal patterns of interaction that support the problems and the underlying marital paradigm concerning roles.

This technique is begun by asking that both spouses initially focus on themselves. A short discussion of roles and their function in the marital relationship is presented to give the couple a frame in which to work. The roles that couples are typically involved in are work/profession, individual, couple, family and extended family, parenting, and household. Both spouses are given a blank circle and asked to draw lines to create pie-shaped pieces on the paper to illustrate how much time they spend fulfilling each role. Encouraging the spouses to focus on their own perceptions of time spent in different roles, rather than their spouse's, is a first step in altering the unproductive patterns of blame, anger, and guilt.

Next, the couple is asked to complete another pie outline, filling in pieces that depict their perception of the other's roles and time spent in these roles. Now the process is tapping into the perception of the other in marital roles. Once the couple has completed these two perception pies, the therapist will individually process the experience with them. It is important for the spouses to listen and refrain from comment while the other is sharing his or her perceptions with the therapist. One of the first questions to be asked is, "How did you feel about doing this exercise?" Usually the respondent that feels the most blamed or the least willing to change will give the most neutral or negative feedback. Responses such as "It was okay" or "I don't see what this has to do with anything" are typical. The spouse with the most desire or initiative for change will typically respond in more positive ways. Other questions to ask are, "What surprises or new information did you become aware of by doing this exercise?" "What do you see as differences in your spouse's and your role allocations?" and "Is there anything you would like to do or think you might need to do differently concerning time spent in different roles?"

The final part of the intervention is future oriented. The couple is asked to use the information from all the pie drawings and jointly develop and illustrate a pie with pieces that would show what a perfect pie for their relationship would look like. This part of the exercise can be done in session or as a homework exercise.

Conclusion

What I have found most interesting about this exercise is couples' responses to visual representation of the roles they are fulfilling. Many times they are astounded to see how much time they perceive themselves or their spouses as functioning in different roles. One spouse actually decided to give up one of his part-time jobs when he saw that both he and his wife's depiction of his work role revealed a slice that took up over three fourths of the pie. Other times the pies have led to a greater understanding of why one of the spouses may feel angry or stressed. However, the most frequent outcome to this intervention is an opening for discussion about role allocation and role overload. For many couples, this is the first time they have actually looked at the roles they fulfill in their relationship and taken time to listen to the other's perceptions.

References

Constantine, L. L. (1984). Dysfunction and failure in open family systems: II. Clinical implications. *Journal of Marital and Family Therapy, 10,* 1–17.

Constantine, L. L. (1986). *Family paradigms: The practice of theory in family therapy.* New York: Guilford Press.

Constantine, L. L., & Israel, J. T. (1985). The family void: Treatment and theoretical aspects of the synchronous family paradigm. *Family Process, 24,* 525–547.

Kantor, D., & Lehr, W. (1975). *Inside the family.* San Francisco: Jossey-Bass.

Nugent, M., & Constantine L. L. (1988). Marital paradigms: Compatibility, treatment, and outcome in marital therapy. *Journal of Marital and Family Therapy, 14,* 351–369.

Reiss, D. (1981). *The family's construction of reality.* Cambridge, MA: Harvard University Press.

∎ ∎ ∎

PART **II**

TRANSGENERATIONAL TECHNIQUES

P art II presents techniques beginning with a transgenerational orientation. The authors integrate additional perspectives into the transgenerational point of departure. Chapter 10, by Marsha Wiggins Frame, explains how to help clients become more aware of and sensitive to the role and impact of their religious/spiritual family history through construction of a religious/spiritual genogram and how to use narrative techniques to develop more greater texture to the genogram. Alan Hovestadt, in chapter 11, discusses how counselors can use a scale that assesses perceived levels of health in one's family of origin to help couples better understand similarities and dissimilarities in their respective family-of-origin experiences. Chapter 12, by Robert Sherman, presents a method for charting transgenerational patterns of intimate behavior by questioning couples about their definitions of intimacy and how intimacy was and is experienced and expressed historically in the family. The final chapter of Part II is an exercise developed by Sherry Gallagher Warden that helps clients move from an "other-blaming" focus and develop a greater sense of self.

10

Constructing Religious/ Spiritual Genograms

Marsha Wiggins Frame, PhD

One of the most practical tools for marriage and family therapy has been the genogram (McGoldrick & Gerson, 1985). In its basic form, the genogram functions as a multigenerational blueprint, or family tree. From this simple diagram, counselors and clients alike are able to view simultaneously family composition, gender, age, ethnicity, dates of birth, marriages, divorces, deaths, and other important family events. In addition, intergenerational therapists have used the genogram to map the transmission of problems across generations (Guerin, 1976). The technique has been particularly useful for therapists in educating their clients about family patterns and in reducing emotional reactivity among family members (Kuehl, 1995).

Religious/Spiritual Issues in Counseling

A major challenge for many marriage and family counselors involves dealing with clients' religious or spiritual beliefs and practices. Recent surveys indicate that most Americans believe in God and that 75% describe themselves as religious (Cadwallader, 1991). Nevertheless, for a variety of reasons, some counselors feel overwhelmed by such clients. It may be that counselors feel incompetent to address religious and spiritual issues in counseling due to their lack of training in this area (Collins, Hurst, & Jacobson, 1987; Genia, 1994; Shafranske & Malony, 1990). Or perhaps counselors view the religious and spiritual realm as nonscientific at best or possibly pathological (Butler, 1990; Prest & Keller, 1993). In addition, counselors' own assumptions about the nature and importance of religion, as well as their personal religious or spiritual experiences, may color their attitude toward working with religious clients (Stander, Piercy, MacKinnon, & Helmeke, 1994). Regardless of the explanations for some counselors' discomfort with their clients' religious or spiritual issues, it is clear that for those who choose to work with religious or spiritual issues in counseling some specific strategies are needed.

The Religious/Spiritual Genogram

The primary purpose of the religious/spiritual genogram is to enable clients to become more aware of and sensitive to the religious or spiritual histories, beliefs, and experiences that shaped their families of origin and to gain insight into how these patterns affect other issues in the couple or family unit. Another aim of this special type of genogram is to incorporate social constructionist principles in working with clients for whom religious and spiritual issues are central. The genogram enables the counselor to focus on the clients' reality as expressed in religious or spiritual "stories" and how these stories can be reauthored (Parry & Doan, 1994) to minimize client distress and maximize well-being. The genogram also aids counselors in helping clients "externalize the problem" (White & Epston, 1990) so that issues with religious or spiritual dimensions can be viewed from outside the self, thus reducing emotional reactivity.

The Basic Genogram

The first step of building the religious/spiritual genogram is to have clients map the family structure by drawing a three-generational genogram, including as much information as possible about family members: grandparents, parents, aunts, uncles, cousins, siblings, nieces, and nephews. Next, significant events and their dates, such as births, marriages, divorces, remarriages, and deaths, should be included. Then a delineation of family relationships can be added. McGoldrick and Gerson (1985) suggested a set of symbols that have become standard in the construction of basic genograms. In addition to denoting gender, identified patient, adoption, stillbirth, abortion, twins, unmarried couples, and deaths, the quality of family relationships can be symbolized as well. Conflict, closeness, distance, and cutoff relationships should be encoded on the genogram.

Adding Religious/Spiritual Information

Lewis (1989) suggested adding color coding to the standard genogram to indicate specific traits or characteristics of family members related to clinical issues. In the religious/spiritual genogram, colors indicate family members' religious traditions. For example, Roman Catholics may be designated in red, Jews in blue, Muslims in orange, Mormons in gray, Buddhists in purple, Protestants in yellow, Unitarians in black, no religious affiliation in brown, agnostic or atheist in pink, and personal spirituality in green. If religious/spiritual background is unknown, no color is added. If a particular family's genogram includes only Protestant Christians, for example, the color code may be changed or expanded to include various denominations: Baptist, Presbyterian, United Methodist, Pentecostal, United Church of Christ, or others. Lightly coloring these designations indicates minimal participation in the religion or spiritual approach. Heavy coloring indicates strong participation in the religious/spiritual orientation. The color-coding process portrays well interreligious marriages across generations.

The colors graphically illustrate the myriad of religious backgrounds that impact clients in fascinating ways. In fact, some couple or family conflicts whose source was outside the clients' awareness become increasingly evident as they view their religious and spiritual histories as depicted on the genogram.

Dates of significant personal religious events should be recorded on the genogram. For example, baptisms, first communions, confirmations, ordinations, bar and bat mitzvahs and other rituals and rites of passage could be included. In addition, for families whose members have been very active in religious organizations, dates of important events in the religious community should be noted. These events might include the death of a well-loved priest, building projects, movement of a congregation to a new location, sexual misconduct of a clergy person leading to dismissal, changing racial/ethnic/class composition in the congregation, or others.

Placing brackets around certain family members indicates that these individuals left a religious/spiritual organization or movement. For family members who convert to other religions or join other types of churches, mosques, or synagogues, clients add another layer of color around the family member's symbol, indicating the specific nature of the change. Dates for leaving and joining religious organizations should be indicated. This dimension of the genogram serves to underscore the stability or fluidity of religious/spiritual affiliation.

Religious or spiritual closeness between family members can be illustrated with several asterisks. Perhaps all members of a large extended family are devout Roman Catholics who attend Mass daily. In this family, religion may be the bond that maintains closeness across generations. Or perhaps the absence of any identified religion or spiritual practice is the cornerstone for a family whose beliefs include independent thinking and self-reliance. These beliefs may have been central for this family who raised their children in a predominantly Protestant, Bible-believing community.

Religious or spiritual conflict between family members can be designated by several caret symbols (^). Perhaps there is conflict between a mother and daughter that occurred when the daughter married outside of her religion. Or perhaps a grandfather left the church as a result of his rejection of that church's core beliefs. His leaving may have created conflict with his wife (grandmother) who continued to be very devout. This representation on the genogram can be extremely revealing. Many times it becomes apparent to clients that discord between family members is buttressed by religious/spiritual friction or disagreements. When such antagonism among family members is depicted, it is helpful for counselors to ask clients to describe the nature of the conflict. Counselors make notations on the genogram as clients explain the specifics. When differing beliefs are the root of the disharmony, those are recorded as succinctly as possible. Counselors can then ask clients about the extent to which these conflicts are being maintained in their current couple or family relationships.

Adding Texture to the Genogram

With the standard genogram in place, enhanced by religious and spiritual dimensions, counselors are postured to expand the information contained in the genogram through careful client questioning. Counselors record client responses. The following questions elicit additional information about the role and function of religion and spirituality in couples and families. They enable counselors and clients to discover the ways in which religious or spiritual beliefs, experiences, rituals, and practices are connected to clients' thera-

peutic issues. In addition, these questions may help clients externalize religious issues and thus reduce emotional tension in their
relationships.

1. What role did religion/spirituality play in your life when you
   were growing up? What role does it play now?
2. What specific religious/spiritual beliefs do you consider most
   important for you now? How are those beliefs a source of closeness or conflict between you and other family members?
3. What religious/spiritual rituals did you participate in as a child
   or adolescent? How important were they in your family? Which
   ones do you still engage in? Which ones have you let go? What
   new rituals have you adopted as an adult? How do these rituals connect to your religious/spiritual belief system?
4. What did/does your religious/spiritual tradition say about gender? About ethnicity? About sexual orientation? How have these
   beliefs affected you and your extended family?
5. What patterns of behavior and relationship resulting from re-
   ligion/spirituality emerge for you as you study your genogram?
   How are you maintaining or diverting from those patterns in
   your current household?
6. How does your religious/spiritual history connect with your
   current distress? What new solutions may occur to you on the
   basis of these discoveries?

Conclusion

The religious/spiritual genogram is a tool that builds on the universal symbols of the standard genogram, but introduces multigenerational religious/spiritual traditions. Clients are able to signify their
religious backgrounds and beliefs, sources of conflict and closeness, and significant events within the family or religious organization. By mapping these experiences and relationships, clients are
enabled to make connections between their presenting problems
and family religious/spiritual history.

References

Butler, K. (1990). Spirituality reconsidered. *The Family Therapy Networker*,
14, 26–37.
Cadwallader, E. (1991). Depression and religion: Realities, perspectives,
and directions. *Counseling and Values*, *35*, 83–92.

Collins, J. R., Hurst, J. C., & Jacobson, J. K. (1987). The blind spot extended: Spirituality. *Journal of College Student Personnel, 28,* 274–276.

Genia, V. (1994). Secular psychotherapists and religious clients: Professional considerations and recommendations. *Journal of Counseling and Development, 72,* 395–398.

Guerin, P. J. (1976). *Family therapy: Theory and practice.* New York: Gardner Press.

Kuehl, B. (1995). The solution-oriented genogram: A collaborative approach. *Journal of Marital and Family Therapy, 21,* 239–250.

Lewis, K. G. (1989). The use of color-coded genograms in family therapy. *Journal of Marital and Family Therapy, 15,* 169–176.

McGoldrick, M., & Gerson, R. (1985). *Genograms in family assessment.* New York: Norton.

Parry, A., & Doan, R. E. (1994). *Story re-visions: Narrative therapy in the postmodern world.* New York: Guilford Press.

Prest, L. A., & Keller, J. F. (1993). Spirituality and family therapy: Spiritual beliefs, myths and metaphors. *Journal of Marital and Family Therapy, 19,* 137–148.

Shafranske, E. P., & Malony, H. N. (1990). Clinical psychologists' religious and spiritual orientations and their practice of psychotherapy. *Psychotherapy, 27,* 72–78.

Stander, V., Piercy, F. P., MacKinnon, D., & Helmeke, K. (1994). Spirituality, religion and family therapy: Competing or complementary worlds? *The American Journal of Family Therapy, 22,* 27–41.

White, M., & Epston, D. (1990). *Narrative means to therapeutic ends.* New York: Norton.

■ ■ ■

11

Unresolved Couple Conflict: Clinical Use of the Family of Origin Scale

Alan J. Hovestadt, EdD

Relatively few people are aware of how they continue to be in fluenced and controlled in their behavior by the unachieved goals and the unresolved problems of the parental and grandparental generations. (Williamson, 1978, p. 94)

Bowen (1978), Framo (1992), and Williamson (1981) suggested that mental health clinicians need to help clients develop an understanding of the connection between past and present couple and family relationships. Clinicians who use various forms of family-of-origin therapy would argue that one of the best and most meaningful means of modifying influences of the family of origin on present behavior is to actively work on these issues in relation to one's family of origin. This chapter illustrates one specific intervention strategy that can be used within the context of couple therapy.

The Family of Origin Scale (FOS; Hovestadt, Anderson, Piercy, Cochran, & Fine, 1985) is a self-report scale of 40 items designed to provide a global assessment of perceived levels of health in one's family of origin. Research using the FOS is widely reported in the professional literature but relatively less has been written about how it can be applied to couple therapy. The theoretical underpin-

nings of the FOS were based on the health model developed by the
research team of Lewis, Beavers, Gossett, and Phillips (1976). The
FOS incorporates 10 theoretical constructs of healthy family functioning: clarity of expression, responsibility, respect for others, open-
ness to others, acceptance of separation and loss, range of feelings,
mood and tone, conflict resolution, empathy, and trust. Each of these
elements of healthy family functioning is represented by 4 items, 2
positively and 2 negatively stated.

Its brevity and ease of administration and scoring enhance the
utility of the FOS. Most clients can complete the scale in less than
15 minutes. The developers of the FOS have suggested that clinical
use of the FOS with either individuals or couples can alert the individual to the possibility that unresolved issues from the past may
play a role in current unresolved conflict, problems, or dysfunctional interpersonal relationships.

Case Example

This particular illustration highlights the potential benefits of using
the FOS with couples in therapy by assisting partners to become
aware of similarities and dissimilarities in their respective family-
of-origin experiences. Bobbie and Carl (pseudonyms) sought marital therapy after a particularly angry and emotionally volatile
argument triggered by the need to make a decision about their 14-
year-old son's high school educational placement. During 15 years
of marriage, the couple had sought couples therapy on four occasions with different therapists. Carl's complaints about the relationship involved Bobbie's inability to express her thoughts and feelings.
He described her as cold, withdrawn, and distant. Bobbie in turn
perceived Carl as angry, hostile, punishing, and bordering on verbally abusive.

Both partners were committed to the marriage but expressed great
dissatisfaction with recurrent troubling and disturbing cycles. Carl
would engage Bobbie in a discussion on an emotionally charged
topic and at some point trigger a sense of fear in Bobbie, causing
her to withdraw emotionally and physically from the situation. Her
distancing infuriated Carl, who continued to pursue her more aggressively, often with a louder tone of voice and somewhat harsher
words. Bobbie felt compelled to further distance herself from her
husband and the emotional tension. Ultimately, they would not speak
to each other for a day to a week, followed by a period of "business
talk" that was totally devoid of any intimacy. There was no shared

sexual intimacy during these periods. Subsequent to the business talk, Bobbie would feel safe and secure, thus allowing her to initiate tentative contact with her mate. Carl readily admitted that he simply waited for her to approach him out of concern that his premature reaching out for intimacy would be intolerable for Bobbie. Eventually, the couple would reunite for a period of weeks or even months, but inevitably the cycle would repeat itself.

Using the FOS

At the conclusion of the third session, the therapist initiated a brief inquiry and discussion about the respective family-of-origin histories of the couple. He suggested that during the next two sessions the couple explore their family-of-origin histories.

After explaining the rationale and method of making a genogram to map the structure of the family, gather information about family members, and examine interpersonal relationships in the family, the therapist invited each partner to take the FOS. He introduced the purpose of the scale as a means to help one recall how well his or her family of origin functioned. After reviewing the standard directions, the therapist reminded each partner that he or she was to respond to the questions as he or she perceived his or her family-of-origin relationships and not to share this information with the other spouse at this time. The therapist indicated that he would score their responses for discussion during a future session. The clients returned their completed questionnaires in separate sealed envelopes.

The fourth session was used to explore Carl's family of origin, and the fifth session, Bobbie's. After basic genograms were constructed in Sessions 4 and 5, the therapist shared the results of the FOS, plotting Bobbie and Carl's scores on the same profile sheet. The results seemed to illuminate the differences in the couple's family-of-origin histories (see Figure 11.1). Although most scores were mid-range, falling between 9 and 15, there was a significant 9-point discrepancy in the range of feelings construct. The therapist encouraged Bobbie to explore her family relationships further. Using a variety of strategies, including a visit with her widowed mother (her father had died 2 years earlier), Bobbie found a number of links between her present relationship difficulties and her family-of-origin experiences. Bobbie described her parents as never having an argument or disagreement that involved emotional expressiveness. Her mother, a homemaker, never raised her voice at her husband or children. Her father, an insurance salesman, had

FIGURE 11.1
Bobbie and Carl's Family of Origin profiles scale.

Profile

Therapists who wish to complete a profile should first record the client's total score for each construct in the row or boxes below. Then place an X on the dot indicating the total score for that construct. A line to connect the Xs should then be drawn. Interpretation of perceived health in the family of origin: low, 4–8; average/midrange, 9–15; high, 16–20. For this comparison, Bobbie is denoted with ■s, and Carl is denoted with ●s.

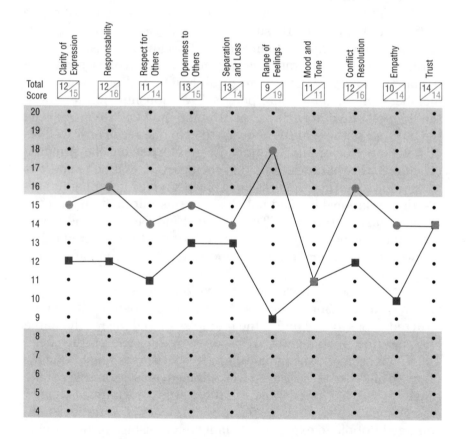

a drinking problem. Her mother was quiet and stoic, tolerating a loveless marriage "because of the kids." During the seventh counseling session, Bobbie revealed unexpectedly and spontaneously that she had a memory of a time when her parents placed their developmentally disabled younger brother in a residential treatment program. Bobbie, as a coparent with her mother, was overcome by sadness and grief and sought solace, comfort, and understanding from her parents. She described them as "numb" and "mute" and totally unable to allow or encourage her expression of feelings. She felt great anger and frustration with her parents that remained in the present.

Carl's family of origin was almost the opposite. Both positive and negative expressions of feelings were well tolerated by his mother, father, and six siblings. Family members would be joyful, happy, sad, angry, anxious, or fearful and know their feelings would be heard, validated, and accepted. After an additional two sessions, the couple reported that they had a small disagreement. Both reported feeling less tense and anxious. Bobbie, over a subsequent period of therapy, worked through unresolved issues with her deceased father, her mother, and her developmentally disabled brother. As she resolved these issues, she became more confident, competent, and tolerant of her own feelings and those expressed by Carl. She found less and less need to retreat from emotionally hot issues in their marriage and indicated that she felt much more able to identify and express her own feelings.

Carl no longer needed to aggressively pursue Bobbie, yet he still struggled with his own willingness to "stay with an issue." When he anticipated that Bobbie would retreat from a hot issue, he was not required to test his commitment to resolve a conflict or problem. As Bobbie's ability to stay with an emotionally charged issue increased, Carl acknowledged some ambivalence about doing the necessary couple work to resolve the concern. Carl also realized that one reason he aggressively pursued her was because he felt he was "losing" an argument when Bobbie retreated. He found a certain satisfaction in knowing that as long as they both worked on an issue, there were no losers but only winners.

Conclusion

The FOS can help each partner in a couple relationship better understand the similarities and differences in their respective family-of-origin experiences. In working with conflicted couples, the FOS can be used by counselors to suggest a relationship between unresolved family-of-origin issues and current conflict in the couple's relationship.

References

Bowen, M. (1978). *Family therapy in clinical practice.* New York: Jason Aronson.

Framo, J. L. (1992). *Family of origin therapy: An intergenerational approach.* New York: Brunner/Mazel.

Hovestadt, A. J., Anderson, W. T., Piercy, F. P., Cochran, S. W., & Fine, M. (1985). A family of origin scale. *Journal of Marital and Family Therapy, 11,* 287–297.

Lewis, J. M., Beavers, W. R., Gossett, J. T., & Phillips, V. A. (1976). *No single thread: Psychological health in family systems.* New York: Brunner/Mazel.

Williamson, D. S. (1978). New life at the graveyard: A method of therapy for individuation from a dead parent. *Journal of Marriage and Family Counseling, 4,* 93–101.

Williamson, D. S. (1981). Personal authority via termination of the intergenerational hierarchical boundary: A "new" stage in the family life cycle. *Journal of Marital and Family Therapy, 7,* 441–452.

■ ■ ■

12

The Intimacy Genogram

Robert Sherman, EdD

The genogram is a popular technique in family therapy that has been described by McGoldrick and Gerson (1985); Sherman and Fredman (1986); and Sherman, Oresky, and Rountree (1991), among others. Geometric figures, lines, and words are used to portray the transgenerational patterns of relationship in the family. Sample charts are provided in the preceding sources, along with explanations of the symbols.

The genogram is a highly adaptable technique. In addition to charting the general family constellation, it can be used for other specific purposes, such as concentrating on vocational and career development; dealing with sexual relations; joining with clients; searching for significant events; and, as described here, finding patterns of intimacy. Counselors encounter a variety of problems and issues among couples and families that inhibit, confuse, or impair intimacy in their relationships. Issues may center on territoriality, intensity of expression, styles of behavior, symbiotic attunement, power and control, sexuality, gender differences, fears, poor communication, and lack of attention or interest in others.

A personal language emerges from the meanings assigned by a person to the life experiences of intimacy, based largely on what

---

Portions of this chapter are taken from *The Family Journal, 1*, 91–93, 1995. © ACA. Used by permission.

was most appealing and what was missing or negative about relationships growing up. These become individual needs that the person strives to satisfy throughout life.

The Intimacy Genogram is a method for charting transgenerational patterns of intimate behavior by questioning clients about their definitions of intimacy and how that intimacy is and was experienced and expressed historically in the family. Doing the genogram helps the couple or family members to understand their respective languages and increases mutual trust and tolerance. Being able to simultaneously think, hear, and see patterns emerge as the genogram is constructed is itself a valuable intimate experience for the couple or family. It helps them and the counselor to assess the differences that are upsetting and normalize them as differences rather than as hostile acts.

Procedures for Constructing an Intimacy Genogram

Hang up a large sheet of white posterboard or newsprint and suggest to clients that it would be useful to find out something about their backgrounds to better understand and solve the current problem, which may in part be influenced by their differences in background. Begin with the person who is most likely to be forthcoming.

Asking Who Questions

The counselor may ask, "Could you tell me who lived together in the family residence? Name all the people who lived with you." This can be followed with questions exploring who is emotionally closest to whom, does the most with whom or for whom, talks about personal experiences and feelings to whom, and is most responsible for initiating intimate relations? Who is the most distant, the most private, or the most emotionally intense or dramatic person? In the case of divorced or remarried families, plot relationships with all pertinent people before and after the divorce or remarriage.

Asking How Questions

The counselor may ask clients about issues such as how distance is established and physical space is used. He or she can also inquire how each person asserts him- or herself or shows anger, sadness, joy, confusion, sympathy, or agreement. How often does intimate behavior occur?

Asking What Questions

The counselor may ask questions such as the following: What kind of personal information and feelings can you share with whom? What does a person have to do concretely in this family so that others will know that he or she is being intimate? What is expected of men and women in this family? What are the rules about being intense and dramatic versus cool and calm? What is private and what is sharable in feelings, beliefs, things, belongings, and physical space—that is, are doors to be open or shut, is one allowed to ask personal questions of another or must one wait to be invited to discuss matters?

Asking When Questions

The counselor may ask questions exploring when intimacy occurs—in bed, at meals, while walking, when scheduled, spontaneously? Does intimacy occur most frequently during fights or during quiet times? Are intimate feelings aired most often in private between two people, before the assembled family, during social gatherings, or only during vacations free of the normal pressures of daily life?

Asking Where Questions

The counselor may query as follows: Where or in what environment is it most comfortable for intimacy to occur—a special room of the home, in the car, at a gathering, in a parent's home, or in a hotel room?

Record individual behavior under each person's name on the chart. Write general family customs and rules at the bottom of the chart.

All responses are analyzed to discover the transgenerational interaction patterns of the couple or family and to discover the rules and assumptive values and expectations concerning intimacy that inform each person's actions in the system. The general family rules at the bottom of the chart are helpful in assessing the major themes and priorities under which they operate. The clients and counselor together analyze the genogram; identify the patterns and rules of intimacy; identify what is permissible and expected of men, women, and children; and conclude in what way they now understand their own interactions and the feelings resulting from them.

They can clearly observe the patterns of behavior from the families of origin that are being imitated, sought after, or guarded against.

They then establish goals for any changes they think will be useful in accommodating difference and expanding their vocabularies of intimate behavior. Issues of trust and safety will often come up, and pursuer–distancer patterns will need to be addressed.

Conclusion

The Intimacy Genogram is a means of creating a visual representation of transgenerational patterns of intimate behavior in the family. The technique helps counselors and clients understand the meaning of intimacy from each partner's respective family-of-origin perspective and helps counselors normalize family-of-origin differences in couples and family counseling.

References

McGoldrick, M., & Gerson, R. (1985). *Genograms in family assessment.* New York: Guilford Press.
Sherman, R., & Fredman, N. (1986). *Handbook of structured techniques in marriage and family therapy.* New York: Brunner/Mazel.
Sherman, R., Oresky, P., & Rountree, Y. (1991). *Solving problems in couples and family therapy: Techniques and tactics.* New York: Brunner/Mazel.

■ ■ ■

13

Self-Focus Exercise

Sherry A. Gallagher Warden, PhD

Many couples who present for therapy engage in a good amount of projection. They deal with conflict mainly by blaming, criticizing, disowning responsibility, and mindreading (i.e., assuming they know what the other is thinking, feeling, and doing). Even though couples say they care about one another and are committed to "staying and working it out," some couples describe themselves as feeling lost and helpless to know what to do to change the relationship. Assuming that the therapist can stay disentangled from the couple's feelings of helplessness, he or she can begin to track their repetitive patterns and cycles. Often both partners might be indicating nonverbally that "if you change first then I'll change—only then will our relationship get better."

Malone and Malone (1987) described the aforementioned exchange as one of the most destructive myths that we can encounter as therapists. "The bilateral myth," as the authors named it, refers to the fact that couples lose touch with the unilateral power that each one has in a relationship: "the power and effectiveness of the I experience and the importance of staying in charge of one's *self* in relationship" (Malone & Malone, 1987, p. 40).

Having clients focus on the self by taking the "I stand" is not new to the field of marriage and family therapy. The concept of the differentiation of self is the principle subject of Bowen's (1976) theory. This concept describes the degree of fusion or differentiation between emotional and intellectual functioning in people. At the low extreme are individuals whose emotions and intellect are so fused that their lives are dominated by their emotional system and can be described as less flexible, less adaptable, and more emotionally dependent. Other aspects of the differentiation of self concept are the levels of solid self and pseudoself within a person. They get their emotional needs met by living their lives through another person. Bowen (1976) posited that in periods of emotional intimacy, two pseudoselves fuse into each other, one losing self to the other, who then gains self. Conversely, the solid self does not participate in the fusion phenomenon. Bowen (1976) described the solid self as "who I am, what I believe, what I stand for and what I will and will not do" (p. 68). The solid self is made up of clearly defined principles, beliefs, and convictions. Couples who possess more pseudo than solid self might react to being asked to make a personal change by saying "Okay, I will do what you want (and I will end up resenting you for it), but you had better do what I want you to do for me."

Bowen (1976) also believed that partners who choose each other possess similar levels of differentiation. Therapists often encounter couples who are equally emotional and overreactive to one another in conflict situations. They are unable to separate their emotions from their logic and thus continue the repetitive cycle of blaming, criticizing, mindreading, and disowning responsibility for self. One partner, tired of arguing, might give in or acquiesce to the other simply to suspend the conflict. However, in neither of these cases is there any conflict resolution or any progress toward more differentiation of self.

Case in Point

I had been working with a couple in their mid-30s who had been together about 2 years. Both were recovering substance abusers and were from dysfunctional families. Each had experienced individual therapy prior to seeing me and continued to attend Alcoholics Anonymous meetings. They were experts at analyzing themselves and each other but were unable to discuss conflict and resolve it productively. The moment a real issue emerged, each one experienced a great deal of anxiety. They both put up their protective armor and became embedded in their cycle of projection, usually distancing from each other. They threw up their hands and looked to me as if to say, "This is hopeless—please tell us what to do!" I pointed out their patterns of relating and asked them to do something different, but to no avail. I then did something different—I self-disclosed about how I took a risk in a new relationship by letting myself be vulnerable, dropping my guard and trusting my partner and myself. I asked them if they would be willing to try this by participating in an exercise of self-focus. This seemed to be one of the turning points in their therapy.

Self-Focus Exercise Procedure

At the beginning of the session, the therapist announces to the couple that she or he will be jotting down some statements during the session that will be shared with them before the session ends. As the session is winding down, the therapist might introduce the procedure in the following manner:

> John and Mary, I notice that each of you seem to be an expert in analyzing the other to determine exactly what the other can do to make this relationship better. You each seem to have good advice for the other to help that person to make some changes. The problem that I see with this strategy is that it prevents you from being completely who you are, the genuine you, the best self you can bring to this relationship. I'd like to propose an exercise that would shift the focus from each other to yourselves. (I like to get both partners' agreement to participate in this exercise before proceeding.)

The therapist begins sharing the I statements that he or she noted during the session, beginning with one partner and moving to the other, making certain to keep the statements in the present tense and positive and validating. The statements may cluster around the following themes: self-esteem, self-responsibility, assertiveness, strengths, and competencies. For example, some of the statements might read like these:

- I am a competent person.
- I am a lovable and capable person.
- I deserve to be happy.
- I ask for my needs to be met.
- I am responsible for my own behavior.
- Others are responsible for their behavior.
- I know how to have fun.
- I am becoming spontaneous.
- I am a good worker.
- I am a good lover.

- I am a good cook, housekeeper, entertainer, decorator, and so on.
- I am a romantic partner.
- I use my creativity to problem solve.

Each partner listens to his or her own list of I statements read by the therapist and is given an opportunity to express his or her thoughts and feelings about hearing the self-validations. My experience has been that people who are not in touch with their feelings and have disowned or denied parts of themselves have an emotional reaction and need time to process these feelings. Additionally, there might be a positive effect on the other partner on hearing validations about his or her mate. The couple is given a homework assignment using the validations. On arising in the morning, they are to read their list of I statements aloud in front of a mirror. I also request that they keep this list with them at all times (in a pocket or purse), adding to the list when they think of a new positive statement. The couple is reminded that if they feel an urge to focus on the other person, they need to bring out their list and reread it as often as necessary to maintain the focus on the self, making certain to keep the I statements positive and in the present tense. I ask them to bring their lists to the next session to discuss their experience during the week.

Conclusion

This procedure can be used with an individual, a couple, a family, or a group. It may be especially useful for clients who feel overresponsible, overprotective, or overinvolved in another person's life at the expense of their own growth and development. Other indications for application of this technique might include individuals who have experienced a delay in the development of a solid sense of self because of abuse (verbal, emotional, physical, or sexual), neglect, dysfunctional family background, or chemical addiction and are unable to experience healthy, intimate relationships.

References

Bowen, M. (1976). Theory in the practice of psychotherapy. In P. J. Guerin (Ed.), *Family therapy: Theory and practice* (pp. 42–60). New York: Gardner Press.

Malone, T. P., & Malone, P. T. (1987). *The art of intimacy.* New York: Simon & Schuster.

■ ■ ■

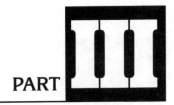

CONSTRUCTIVE TECHNIQUES

Part III consists of techniques from constructivist and social constructionist paradigms. Chapter 14, by James Robert Bitter, explains how counselors can help couples view problems from new perspectives through the use of externalization interviews. In chapter 15, Michael Carns discusses using video or audio feedback within sessions to help clients and the counselor coassess the interactions and patterns of behavior. Phyllis Erdman, in chapter 16, describes how asking each family member to bring an item that symbolizes his or her view of self within the system can help family members share their personal meanings and experiences of being in the family. Chapter 17, by Richard Riordan and Johanna Soet, explains the process and procedures of using various forms of therapeutic writing in couples and family counseling. The final chapter, by William Walsh and Robert Keenan, describes how counselors can share information indirectly with couples and families—without direct inquiry or confrontation—through "therapeutic gossiping."

14

Dissolving a Problem: Structuring Externalization Interviews With Couples

James Robert Bitter, PhD

Problems gain power in the lives of individuals and couples in direct relation to people feeling discouraged, disabled, and without power. When the problem gains total control of the relationship, the problem, the relationship, and the people fuse; they are all experienced and lived as one entity. "We are volatile," "we are avoidant," or "we are disengaged" take on the same singularly defining power as "I am alcoholic," "I am narcissistic," or "I am bulimic." The problem has been given a life, and it has taken over.

If we can resist the urge to provide a quick-fix answer, there are some narrative therapy interviewing strategies, developed by Michael White and David Epston (1990; Epston & White, 1992), that can be used to empower couples who are wrestling with a problem. According to Epston, White, and Murray (1992), narrative therapy is a "reauthoring therapy" that

> intends to assist persons to resolve problems by: (1) enabling them to separate their lives and relationships from knowledge/stories that are impoverishing; (2) assisting them to challenge practices of self and relationship that are subjugating; and (3) encouraging persons to re-author their lives according to alternative knowledge/stories

and practices of self and relationship that have preferred outcomes. (p. 108)

The key to the process of "dissolving a problem" is to ask questions that make it possible for the problem solver to see the difficulty in a new way, to get a hold of resources that have not been used, and to create options not yet considered. In essence, the person having the problem becomes a consultant to the person helping to solve the problem. The answer to the problem is that the people who make up the couple are put back in charge of their own stories. This is the essence of empowering couples.

Starting From a "Not Knowing" Position

An interview for change, one that really seeks to solve problems, almost always starts with an exploration of the problem and the people involved in it. The interviewer assumes that he or she knows nothing about what is happening and wants to find out. The following are information-seeking questions or openers: (a) Tell me everything you know about the problem and what you have done so far; (b) When did the problem start and how do you hope it will end? (c) How is the problem affecting your life? (d) Who else, besides you, is affected by this problem, and in what way? (e) What are you feeling or what is your reaction when you are right in the middle of the problem? or (f) Have you ever had a similar problem, and how did it turn out?

Personifying the Problem

Because the couple takes the problem seriously, it is essential that the problem be addressed. The couple may define the problem as each other: "She's never around" or "He's always nagging me." Couple problems, however, are most often relational, based on patterned interactions constructed over time. These interactions repeat themselves with the force of habit and are experienced as imperatives from which the couple cannot disengage. Asking the couple to name the problem is the first step in disengagement. It may also be one of their first cooperative acts in relation to the problem. Personifying the problem is facilitated by using language that represents the "near" experience of the couple—a definition of the concrete, observable, active movement in their relationship. "The Painful War" says so much more than "we don't agree on much, and we are always fighting." Defining a problem and personifying it puts the couple at a certain distance from the experience of "problem." There is always a separation between the definers and the defined, a standing back, a movement away, a place to breathe.

Externalizing the Problem

Too often, couples become immobilized by a problem because they have begun to see their difficulties and themselves as one and the same. Instead of being people who overuse temper, for example, they think of themselves as bad tempered with little or nothing they can do about it. Here are a few questions that separate the problem from the problem solver: (a) How does the problem get you involved with it? (b) How does the problem get you to take part in its mischief? (c) How does the problem catch you off guard and surprise you before you know what is happening? (d) How does the problem fool you into thinking it is important, necessary, or beneficial? or (e) What price does the problem demand from you, how does it exact the price, and how does it make itself look worth it?

Unique Outcomes

No matter what kind of problem a couple faces, they have usually had at least one similar problem that they solved or that worked out. Finding that unique event is the key to the next step of the interview: (a) Was there ever a time when you resisted the problem, sidestepped it, or just didn't get caught up in it? (b) What led to that breakthrough? (c) What resources were you using? (d) What advice did you give yourself? (e) What were the key steps? or (f) What had happened in your history that prepared you for your handling of the problem?

Unique Possibilities

If the negative experiences are used to confirm the experience of "having a problem," then unique outcomes can be used to create a sense of being able to handle problems. Questions posing these possibilities include the following: (a) Knowing what you now know about your ability to handle difficulties, how will this affect your next step? (b) How do you think you will feel taking the next step? (c) How will that feeling affect your actions and how you see yourselves and each other? (d) What resources will you need this time, and how will you make sure you have them with you? or (e) Imagine this problem is solved by you in a week or month or whatever it takes. Looking back with hindsight, what are the steps that were most significant in handling this?

Celebrating the Problem Solvers

Here are a few final questions that make a problem handled a valued experience: (a) Besides me, who else would not be surprised that you figured out an answer to this problem? (b) What would it be like for them to hear from you? (c) Do you think it would be helpful to catch others up on what you have figured out? (d) Who should know? or (e) What would be a good way to celebrate this solved problem so that it can be remembered in the future? These questions have the effect of returning the couple to the larger "family" that knows and supports them. They create avenues by which the couple's system is experienced as embedded in their own therapeutic community. It is the discovery that people are not alone in their struggles that gives strength.

Conclusion

The process of structuring externalizing interviews evolved over time in the collaborations of Epston and White (1992). When one watches these master therapists at work, they do not always follow a given step-by-step process. They will leave their structure when part or all of it does not fit the needs of clients or the therapeutic situation. Nevertheless, structure is often a useful initial support for learning anything new.

References

Epston, D., & White, M. (1992). *Experience, contradiction, narrative, and imagination: Selected papers of David Epston and Michael White (1989–1994)*. Adelaide, South Australia, Australia: Dulwich Center.

Epston, D., White, M., & Murray, K. (1992). A proposal for re-authoring therapy: Rose's revisioning of her life and a commentary. In S. McNamee & K. J. Gergen (Eds.), *Therapy as social construction* (pp. 96–115). Newbury Park, CA: Sage.

White, M., & Epston, D. (1990). *Narrative means to therapeutic ends*. New York: Norton.

■ ■ ■

15

Using Audio and
Video Feedback

Michael R. Carns, PhD

An important aspect of couples and family counseling is acquaint-
ing clients with the process that they use to solve problems.
Typically, clients come to therapy with little awareness of the problem-solving patterns learned from their families of origin. Watzlawick,
Weakland, and Fisch (1974) stated that a basic component of their
therapy is helping clients to understand the repetitive way they
continue to apply solutions to problems that do not work. One of
their first therapy goals is to move the client from focusing on the
problem to focusing on how they problem solve (Watzalawick et
al., 1974). Murray Bowen's (1978) approach uses genograms to ac-
quaint clients with the multigenerational transmission of attitudes
and values that they use on a daily basis to reduce or eliminate
anxiety-producing situations. In agreement with Watzlawick and
Bowen, I believe a major focus of couples and family counseling
should address developing awareness of the dysfunctional problem-solving patterns and processes that inhibit adaptive interpersonal relationships and interfere with an adaptive self-concept.

As noted by Adlerians, counseling should be a process of empowerment or encouragement of clients (Sherman & Dinkmeyer,
1987). To a large extent, this empowerment comes through an egalitarian and collaborative alliance between the client and the coun-

selor. In this encouraging environment, clients may develop the capacity to observe themselves from a distance. This capacity helps clients to gain a more objective and less defensive posture toward their own situation and toward the therapy process.

Using video and audio feedback (VAF) enhances the process of strengthening clients' self-esteem and their capacity to problem solve effectively. To achieve these goals, couples or families are invited to view or listen to themselves as they interact with the therapist or significant others in session. The VAF format allows clients the opportunity to coassess with counselors as clients are asked to move outside of themselves and view themselves from a distance.

Counselors should discuss the use of video and audiotape when providing informed consent information to clients. If clients strongly object to being either video or audiotaped, their objections should be honored. The use of VAF is typically introduced during the working stage of counseling when the process of coassessment with clients becomes so important. Counselors should briefly discuss—in advance—the VAF process with clients and state that the use of video and audio helps counselors be more effective in counseling. The first feedback tapes are chosen to elicit evaluation and feedback from clients regarding the counseling process and their experience of the counselor. Subsequent tapes include gradually more focus on the clients as they are asked to evaluate themselves.

In my experience, video feedback is more powerful than audio because it provides the most thorough review of that portion of the session. If video is not feasible, audio feedback is still beneficial. When using audio feedback, it is helpful to have two recorders available in session. Often as the counselor and clients listen to the section of the tape together, therapy begins. With two recorders, the counselor is able to switch on the other recorder to record the ensuing interaction.

Procedure and Uses

Sessions using VAF typically last 1.5 hours This provides sufficient time for review of past therapy material through the audio or video presentation, while providing clients sufficient time to share and process new material. Following a discussion of the previous week's homework assignments, the counselor introduces a section of tape from the previous session. The decision of what to review from the previous session is guided by several principles. These include any important statements or behaviors that the counselor may have missed: verbal and nonverbal client responses that indicate the capacity of clients to be fully in touch with their own needs, feelings, and behavior as well as those of others; inconsistencies and incongruities in either the counselor's presentation or that of clients; moments in the session during which one would expect clients to have experienced some negative affect, but they did not share or display it; moments when something confusing happened, and the counselor either missed the confusion or decided that it was inappropriate to address it at that time; and moments that represent overall problem-solving patterns of clients to facilitate their awareness of the patterns.

Tapes may be introduced in the following manner:

> You might recall from our discussion last time that we were talking about how your youngest son does not seem to respond to you as readily as your oldest son. During one part of the interview, we did a role-play together and I asked you to pick a typical area of conflict between you and your youngest son. I then asked you to demonstrate for me how you would go about communicating to him your concerns. I also asked you to role-play what you would say and do as he began to ignore or defy your concerns. I want to play this particular part of the tape where I was playing your son and I began to defy you verbally. I know that we discussed the role-play afterward and we discussed this part of the role-play. In reviewing the video for this week of both this role-play and our discussion that followed the role-play, I did not believe that we really got to the core of the matter that goes on between the two of you when these highly charged emotional interactions occur. In some ways, our discussion following the role-play felt as emotionally charged as the role-play itself. It seemed like we were really missing each other in our communication, very much like what happens between you and your son. So I want to replay a section of the role-play and a section of our discussion after it, if that is okay with you?

This introduction of the tape helps clients focus and empowers them as they take on the role of consultant in solving their problems. The VAF procedure is helpful in avoiding subtle power struggles of silence or verbal prodding to motivate client involvement.

This technique is helpful in a number of other ways. It helps the client move from storytelling to examining process. It provides important insight for clients that their behavior is not just coincidental or random but rather fits a well-defined pattern of responses to stress and anxiety-producing situations. The process of confrontation may become more effective by viewing or listening to an objective element outside of the counselor–client relationship. The use of audio and video feedback may also help counselors examine their own therapy interactions. In my experience, clients more readily identify and discuss their perceptions of me in our interactions when allowed to review it on audio or videotape.

Some situations and categories of client behaviors require caution when applying this technique. Contraindications for use include times of crisis in therapy and when working with clients with severe psychological disorders.

Conclusion

It is not my intention to have the client agree with my perception or interpretation of the section of tape I play for them. It is my intention to produce an enactment or reenactment. I wish to bring an immediacy to therapy that duplicates clients' typical problem-solving process. This allows me to work with individuals, couples, and families in a very real way that relates to their patterns of problem solving outside of therapy.

References

Bowen, M. (1978). *Family therapy in clinical practice*. New York: Jason Aronson.

Sherman, R., & Dinkmeyer, D. (1987). *Systems of family therapy: An Adlerian integration*. New York: Brunner/Mazel.

Watzlawick, P., Weakland, J., & Fisch, R. (1974). *Change: Principles of problem formation and problem resolution*. New York: Norton.

■ ■ ■

16

Bringing a Symbol: An Experiential Exercise for Systemic Change

Phyllis Erdman, PhD

Murray Bowen and Carl Whitaker are two of the pioneers of family therapy whose contributions cannot be underestimated. Bowen's concepts of differentiation and triangulation refer to the importance of individuals taking responsibility for their own change in the system, regardless of whether other members change or not (Kerr & Bowen, 1988). Whitaker and Keith (1981) also emphasized that it is not necessary for everyone in the family to change; what is important is that something be done differently in the family. When one person reacts differently, other members cannot remain the same. This is what Watzlawick, Weakland, and Fisch (1974) referred to as second-order change. It is a change in the system that seems illogical and unpredictable and requires the rules of the system to be altered.

Families often come to therapy with "change me, don't change me" attitudes; and although they want symptomatic behaviors to subside, they really want the system to remain the same (Papp, 1983; Watzlawick et al., 1974). Nichols (1987) warned against the tendency for systemic therapists to overlook the individual's responsibility in changing the system: "Therapists don't change, systems don't change;

people change. To be more exact, therapists initiate change, systems undergo change, but individual persons must make changes" (p. 38).

Because patterns of behavior in families are so resistant to change, an indirect introduction of change through the use of metaphors is sometimes more effective than directives (Barker, 1985). Keith and Whitaker (1981) used metaphors in an experiential manner by introducing the strategy of play with families. Play is a way to combine symbolic meaning and real meaning by shifting back and forth between metaphors and reality during therapy, noting that "change shows itself in posture as well as in a decrease in symptoms" (Keith & Whitaker, 1981, p. 244).

The technique described in this chapter borrows from Bowen's conceptualization of individual responsibility in systemic change (Kerr & Bowen, 1988) and Whitaker's emphasis on the experiential process of therapy (Keith & Whitaker, 1981; Whitaker & Keith, 1981). Additionally, it emphasizes two of the key concepts of a solution focused approach—that only a small amount of change is necessary (Selekman, 1993) and that focusing on how things will be different in the future provides hope and expands the options for solutions (Cade & O'Hanlon, 1993).

"Bringing a Symbol" Procedure

The therapist asks each family member to bring something to the next session that is symbolic of who he or she is in the family but not to tell the other members what they are bringing. The symbol may refer to the role family members play in the family, how they see themselves in relation to other family members, or how they think other family members view them. For instance, a client may bring a sponge because he thinks he absorbs all of the problems in the family and carries all the pain while others are problem free. Or a client might bring a firecracker because she thinks everyone sees her as the explosive member who always upsets the stability of the family. These objects metaphorically represent the client's position and role in the family.

The therapist may explain this request as an attempt to learn what it is like to live in the family from each member's perspective. The request may be especially helpful if the family is vague about what the problem is or if there is not a consensus on what the family members want to have happen in therapy.

During the next session, each member is asked to tell the other members what they have brought and what it symbolizes. The therapist's role during this session is to listen and to clarify. For example, the therapist may ask how large a sponge the family member is, thereby giving a clue to the magnitude of the problem(s) as well as to the client's perceived burden. The therapist acknowledges each family member's responses. The purpose at this point is only to share each family member's experience, so the therapist does not offer an interpretation at this time. At the end of this session, family members are asked to bring a symbol to the next session indicative of their place in the family when change has occurred and, again, not to divulge their symbol in advance. The purpose behind this request is twofold: (a) to help the client focus on the future when the problem no longer exists and (b) to help the client see his or her contribution toward change, regardless of the other family members.

At the next session, family members are again asked to share their symbols. This time, however, they are asked to explain how they will be different and how they think that will affect other members. For example, the sponge may become a diamond. The therapist may ask, "When you become a diamond, how will the other members react to you?" The client may respond that everyone else will be envious because of his precious value. Another question may be, "What will happen if your sister/brother/parent doesn't like you as a diamond?" Some members may not choose a new symbol and wish to stay as they are. In this case, the therapist may ask the client, "When you change and become a diamond, do you think the rest of your family will stay the same? What do you think they will become?" The emphasis during this session is on each individual's attempt to change, regardless of its effect on other family members. The questions are meant to validate the client's goals but also to reinforce each individual's responsibility for initiating systemic change from within him- or herself rather than from expectations of other members. This session also focuses on exceptions and solutions—rather than on problems—thus directing clients toward options for change.

The next few sessions may include a variety of interventions and may focus on any aspect of change—behavioral sequences, affective reactions, cognitions, or others. The key is that the therapist, as well as family members, understand at a metaphorical, as well as at a reality level, what it is like to live in this family and what it will be like when change has occurred. The assumption is that change will happen, regardless of who resists it.

Conclusion

The most effective time to use this symbolic technique is during the joining process, while the therapist is trying to connect with each family member and trying to develop a clear understanding of the family's perception of the problem. It is possible that some clients may perceive this technique as trivial, especially if they perceive their problem to be at a critical point. In this case, the therapist will need to provide a rationale that validates their current pain but also instills trust in the therapeutic process.

References

Barker, P. (1985). *Using metaphors in psychotherapy.* New York: Brunner/ Mazel.

Cade, B., & O'Hanlon, W. H. (1993). *A brief guide to brief therapy.* New York: Norton.

Keith, D. V., & Whitaker, C. A. (1981). Play therapy: A paradigm for work with families. *Journal of Marital and Family Therapy, 7,* 243–254.

Kerr, M. E., & Bowen, M. (1988). *Family evaluation.* New York: Norton.

Nichols, M. P. (1987). *The self in the system: Expanding the limits of family therapy.* New York: Brunner/Mazel

Papp, P. (1983). *The process of change.* New York: Guilford Press.

Selekman, M. D. (1993). *Pathways to change.* New York: Guilford Press.

Watzlawick, P., Weakland, J. H., & Fisch, R. (1974). *Change: Principles of problem formation.* New York: Norton.

Whitaker, C. A., & Keith, D. V. (1981). Symbolic–experiential family therapy. In A. S. Gurman & D. P. Kniskern (Eds.), *Handbook of family therapy* (pp. 187–225). New York: Brunner/Mazel.

■ ■ ■

17

Scriptotherapy: Therapeutic Writing for Couples and Families

Richard J. Riordan, PhD
Johanna E. Soet, MA

The use of writing as an adjunct to therapy is not a new practice. In 1942, Gordon Allport was one of the first psychologists to outline the potential therapeutic contributions of client writing. More recently, Riordan (1996) adopted the term *scriptotherapy* as he reviewed the accumulating research in support of therapeutic writing. Scriptotherapy refers to the various forms of writing that may be used in a therapeutic context. This term corresponds well with another adjunct, bibliotherapy, which refers to counselor-guided reading of written materials in support of the therapy. Often these two techniques are used in a complementary way. One form of interactive bibliotherapy combines reading and writing and may use materials such as workbooks that invite a written response.

In couples and family counseling, scriptotherapy has many potential uses for enhancing therapeutic outcomes. Watzlawick, Beavin, and Jackson (1967), for example, described the way a breakdown of verbal communication between two people can lead to a reliance on analogical or nonverbal exchanges. This encrypted form of communication often results in misinterpretation, misunderstandings, and deterioration of the relationship, particularly if trust has been diminished. Scriptotherapy forces communication into an explicit written format that is less open to misinterpretation. Writing slows the pace of communication and allows the couple or family to reflect on their feelings; accurately express themselves; and reciprocally, better understand the meanings of the others.

Theoretical Underpinnings

Theoretical support for the therapeutic benefits of writing comes from many sources. For example, one psychosomatic theory of inhibition postulates that the effort required to repress traumatic and troubling thoughts and feelings produces short-term increases in autonomic nervous system activity (Buck, 1984; Pennebaker, 1990). This increase in activity takes its toll on the body's overall physical system and may increase the probability of stress-related disease. Writing offers an individual the opportunity to cognitively process and gain a sense of control over his or her experiences, which leads to a decrease in stress to the autonomic nervous system.

The benefits of scriptotherapy can also be understood using general learning theory, in which practice and physical activity are considered critical factors in knowledge and skill acquisition (L'Abate, 1992). The physical aspect of writing can assist clients in participating actively in practicing the desired thinking skills that have been discussed and mutually arrived at in previous sessions. Finally, research addressing human communication and change has contributed to our understanding of the benefits of writing in therapy, particularly as it may apply to couples and families. Watzlawick, Weakland, and Fisch (1974) noted that changing some aspect of the event can sometimes alter rigid patterns of ineffective interaction. A shift from talking to writing can allow the interacting parties to reframe situations, generating different perceptions, expectations, and ultimately behaviors.

Although it is derived from a diversity of conceptual bases, scriptotherapy is pantheoretical in that it can be integrated into any counseling approach (Riordan, 1996). Each approach, however, may have slightly different tactical uses for it. For example, a client-centered therapist may use it to encourage exploration and insight. Adlerians may use scriptotherapy to identify mistaken assumptions. For strategic practitioners, scriptotherapy may assist in uncovering those system variables not visible in the session. A cognitive behaviorist may ask clients to practice what they have learned in their therapy by writing.

Applications of Scriptotherapy

Because of scriptotherapy's possibilities for wide application, many issues can be addressed, either directly or adjunctively, with the technique. Riordan (1996) described four areas in detail: (a) unconscious processes and insights, (b) education and communication, (c) trauma and grief, and (d) career and life review and planning. Although all these areas can be addressed in couples and family therapy, education and improved communication have been the most frequent objective of scriptotherapy with these populations. We present only a few of the many possibilities here.

Interactive dialogue journals have been reported to increase the quality of communication between parents and their children and teachers and their students (Farley & Farley, 1987). This technique had the positive effect of slowing the process of communication, allowing for a reestablishment of explicit versus nonverbal language and providing time for exploration and reflection. In this report, the rules of grammar were suspended so that the emphasis would be on communication rather than on structural inhibitions, such as syntax and spelling.

In a similar vein, Rudes (1992) described an intervention using letter exchange with a couple whose communication patterns had become conflictual and rigid. With this approach, couples are asked to write a letter to each other as if they were in the courtship stage, just before they committed to each other. This can help them to revisit the reasons they came together and focus on priorities and the ways they may have changed as a couple.

Writing about the previous session and comparing what each has written can be enlightening in cases in which communication is a question. Yalom (1985), for example, described using written summaries of sessions in working with a young female writer who was experiencing writer's block. He and the young woman wrote candid postsession summaries of what they were thinking or feeling during the session. These summaries were shared and processed after the session. What is often striking about this approach is that, as happened to Yalom, it sometimes feels as if the participants in therapy were in a different room because the accounts can be so different. This technique is very helpful in assisting couples and families to uncover and explore covert issues during therapy.

Finally, another technique that works well with couples and families is scenario writing (Haddock, 1989). One way involves writing a future autobiography as a formalized type of imagery. These scenarios can be used by clients to rewrite narratives or to visualize alternative futures. This is an especially powerful tool for couples in rewriting and reframing their past as well as exploring their visions of a shared or separate future.

Formats of Scriptotherapy

There are different formats for the use of scriptotherapy in counseling couples and families. Structured writing involves detailed assignments that address particular issues in counseling. For example, Shelton and Ackerman (1974) described asking a marital partner who was obsessed by past grievances to compile a "hurt museum." This involved spending several minutes a day writing down all memories of past hurtful events in the marriage. The list is then brought to the next session for resolution.

Workbooks are another form of structured writing or interactive bibliotherapy. These materials combine reading and writing in a psychoeducational format. Workbooks have been created specifically for couples by Stuart and Jacobson (1987) and for families by Doub and Scott (1987).

Programmed writing is a more recent format for scriptotherapy. It is modeled after programmed instruction techniques that were popular with educators in the 1960s and 1970s (L'Abate, 1992). Programmed writing is similar to structured writing but is more targeted, focused, and organized. It consists of self-administered, self-instructional, systematically written lessons done as weekly homework. Among the many lessons described by L'Abate is a program aimed at curtailing verbal abuse. The first lesson has the clients answer structural questions that define in exacting detail what constitutes verbal abuse. The second session has the family review a list of possible explanations for the verbal abuse (e.g., "Being verbally abusive keeps us from getting too close to one another"; L'Abate, 1992, p. 224) and ranking or writing down what explanation applies to them. Then they are asked to write in detail how these acts could be decreased. The third session is prescriptive in setting paradoxical kinds of tasks (e.g., "Use sarcasm, exaggeration and cynicism whenever possible"; L'Abate, 1992, p. 224) to be accomplished at preset, timed meetings for the express purpose of practicing competent abusive behavior. After the session, each family member reviews the audiotape, checks only his or her own notes, and brings the materials to the next session. Clients in scenarios such as this agree to complete the homework by signing an informed consent contract, and they are regularly given feedback on their work. L'Abate considered programmed writing as a way to translate self-help book material into active practice. His book is an excellent source for counselors who want examples of programs or want to design their own programmed writing materials for their clients.

Logistical Issues With Scriptotherapy

The following are some guidelines to assist the practitioner with using scriptotherapy. These are general guidelines that allow for a great deal of flexibility and creativity and should be adapted as the counselor chooses. When starting out, one may wish to follow the guidelines more closely until a unique and comfortable style of scriptotherapy is developed.

1. *Schedule.* Recommend that the writing be done at a set time each day for a specific amount of time. This time can range from 15 minutes to 1 hour, and the frequency can range from every day to once a week. The amount of time given to writing may depend on the issues being addressed in the writing.
2. *Location.* Encourage the clients to write in a location that is free from distraction and will allow him or her to write uninterrupted.
3. *Topic or theme.* Give the clients a sense of focus and direction by suggesting a specific topic for writing. In the beginning, however, clients may benefit from less focus until themes are identified.
4. *Free style.* Encourage the clients to write without regard to rules of grammar, sentence structure, or style, although the counselor can plead for legibility.
5. *Feedback.* Plan a time for feedback. Some options for this include (a) having clients read some of their writing out loud during the session, (b) reading the writing silently during the session, (c) having couples and families exchange the writing and read each other's out loud, (d) reading the clients notes after the session and giving feedback the following session, and (e) providing written feedback. When providing written

feedback, exercise caution. Make your responses clear and unambiguous, preferably encouraging and positive without sacrificing hard realities.

6. *Agreeing on scriptotherapy.* Discuss the possibility of using scriptotherapy early in therapy to reduce any resistance that may occur if it is introduced later in the process.

7. *Client readiness.* Do not assign writing until you are confident that the clients can handle the issues that may arise in the process.

8. *Alternatives.* If a client is unable to write because of a lack of education, a disability, or other reasons, tape recording may work as an alternative to writing.

9. *Differences between writing and talking.* Clients may feel comfortable discussing some issues and writing about others. Using scriptotherapy provides a good opportunity to explore why some things may feel safer written or spoken.

10. *Getting started.* To begin, try this technique with a few selected clients. As you receive feedback, revise your methods.

11. *Monitoring the process.* Watch for any negative effects writing may have on your clients, such as overreliance. Planning for regular feedback should provide the opportunity to monitor the effects of writing on your clients.

Advantages and Disadvantages

We have attempted to outline some of the uses of scriptotherapy with couples and families. It is important to note that all techniques have both advantages and disadvantages. The advantages of scriptotherapy include efficiency of time and task. That is, using scriptotherapy as an adjunct to face-to-face counseling may speed up the process by encouraging clients to work on their own outside of the therapy hour. This technique may also help make the most of the therapy hour because clients will be sending or bringing in material written the previous week to discuss. Scriptotherapy provides physical involvement for the clients (and sometimes the therapist) in the counseling process. Writing forces clients to physically express some of their issues and produce concrete evidence of their part in therapy. The uses and forms of scriptotherapy are continuing to expand, providing counseling practitioners with a wider repertoire of examples from which to draw.

In some situations, scriptotherapy can become problematic. A family or couple may begin to use writing not as a means to improve the relationship but as a way to avoid appropriate verbal communication or action. Scriptotherapy may also lead to obsessive rumination about a particular topic or issue. For these reasons, it is crucial that regular feedback be given to clients regarding their written work. Clarifying the goals of writing—as a way to encourage healthy interaction—can also assist in making scriptotherapy an effective adjunct to counseling.

Conclusion

Scriptotherapy is a relatively new term to describe the growing practice of using writing as an adjunct to therapy. These varied techniques may be particularly useful in working with couples and families to educate and improve communication. Dialogue journals and letter exchange are examples of ways to use scriptotherapy when a couple's or family's patterns of communication have become conflictual and rigid or imbued with underlying meanings that need exploration. Family-of-origin narratives and scenario writing are examples of ways scriptotherapy can be used to educate members of couples or families.

References

Allport, G. W. (1942). *The use of personal documents in psychological science.* New York: Social Science Research Council.

Buck, R. (1984). *Communication of emotion.* New York: Guilford Press.

Doub, G. T., & Scott, V. M. (1987). *Family wellness workbook: Survival skills for the healthy family.* San Jose, CA.

Farley, J. W., & Farley, S. L. (1987). Interactive writing and gifted children: Communication through literacy. *Journal for the Education of the Gifted, 10,* 99–106.

Haddock, B. (1989). Scenario writing: A therapeutic application. *Journal of Mental Health Counseling, 11,* 234–243.

L'Abate, L. (1992). *Programmed writing: A paratherapeutic approach for intervention with individuals, couples and families.* Pacific Grove, CA: Brooks/Cole.

Pennebaker, J. W. (1990). *Opening up: The healing power of confiding in others.* New York: Avon Books.

Riordan, R. J. (1996). Scriptotherapy: Therapeutic writing as a counseling adjunct. *The Journal of Counseling & Development, 74,* 263–269.

Rudes, J. (1992). Interactional letters: A reorganization of a couple's communication. *Journal of Marital and Family Therapy, 18,* 189–192.

Shelton, J. L., & Ackerman, J. M. (1974). *Homework in counseling and psychotherapy: Examples of systematic assignments for therapeutic use by mental health professionals*. Springfield, IL: Charles C. Thomas.

Stuart, R. B., & Jacobson, B. (1987). *Couple therapy workbook*. Champaign, IL: Research Press.

Watzlawick, P., Beavin, J. H., & Jackson, D. D. (1967). *Pragmatics of human communication: A study of interactional patterns, pathologies and paradoxes*. New York: Norton.

Watzlawick, P., Weakland, J. H. & Fisch, R. (1974). *Change: Principles of problem formation and problem resolution*. New York: Norton.

Yalom, I. D. (1985). *The theory and practice of group psychotherapy*. New York: Basic Books.

■ ■ ■

18

Therapeutic Gossip

William M. Walsh, PhD
Robert Keenan, MA

Most therapy situations involve one therapist and one or more clients. This is true in individual, group, or family therapy modalities. However, some situations, in practice as well as in training, use the services of two therapists or one therapist and one therapist in training. This practice seems to be most common in marriage and family therapy. Couples and families are generally flattered by the attention they receive by having two therapists assist them with the obstacles of family life. The professional literature seems to support the notion that four eyes are better than two or that two voices are more powerful than one. Cotherapy teams can exert a stronger, more profound therapeutic force, accounting for greater symptom improvement and shorter lengths of treatment (Knight, 1990).

Gossip is defined as rumor or report of an intimate nature and also as chatty talk. This technique is used primarily in cotherapy situations, but it can be used creatively in single-therapist situations. When used by cotherapists, it is initially a way for the therapists to communicate with each other. However, an alternative reason for its use is to share information with the family or couple without direct inquiry or confrontation. This indirect dialogue often becomes key, particularly after the family is accustomed to the communication between therapists.

Gossiping is not unlike the reflecting teams in narrative therapy (Andersen, 1991; White, 1991, 1993). Following a family session, observers from behind a one-way mirror switch places with the family in the therapy room and discuss multiple perspectives based on their observations. The family curiously watches and listens from behind the mirror. The team raises questions about contradictions to the problem story as well as previously vague but possibly preferred experiences the family members shared during the session. Family members can then select which comments had most meaning for them or best fit their experience. These conversations are extremely valuable in highlighting new narratives versus the "problem saturated narratives."

This type of interchange can be integrated into various models of family therapy. During any session, a family listens and attends to the cotherapist's brief dialogue of thoughts, dynamics, and compliments, frequently with utmost attention. After all, the therapists are discussing their favorite subject . . . them. Family members will usually respond automatically to the gossip in some way, no matter what model of family therapy the group is using.

Gossip can be used in most contexts and with most models coupled with other techniques. The remainder of this chapter is devoted to the many and varied uses of therapeutic gossip.

Normalizing and Reframing

Both normalizing and reframing, components of solution-focused brief therapy, are catalytic to quick change. Regardless of the therapist's preferred model of doing therapy, these ingredients can be added to encourage positive movement in any session. When these methods are used subtly in gossiping situations, even the novice cotherapist team can expect profound effects.

Normalizing happens when the listening therapist validates a family member's position with "me too" style statements. For example, when a mother says, "I am at my wits' end with these calls from the school," the therapist could reply, "I would be, too." This assures the mother that she is not alone or peculiar in her beliefs. This can have a soothing effect on the client, especially in the early stages of therapy, when members are trying to muster up enough bravery to face relational difficulties. It also helps to balance the normalizing throughout the system, so nobody feels left out. The cotherapy team can increase the intensity of this effect with the use of gossip. When cotherapists are from different age ranges, races, or genders, the effects are even more enigmatic. When the client hears agreement and validation from two separate individuals who happen to be credible professionals in the field of therapy, the experience can be uplifting. Keep in mind, nearly anything can be normalized, so caution must be taken to avoid normalizing topics such as family violence, child abuse, drug use, or other unacceptable behaviors.

Reframing is an alternative description of cognitions, events, dynamics, or behaviors that provide clients with new and exciting ways to consider their situations. This leads to more options in generating different, more effective solutions. Cotherapy teams, disclosing dual alternative descriptions, open up even greater possibilities for exploring change. It is essential that the reframe is a close match for the reality of the family, or the family will dismiss the effort as mere patronizing. It is respectful of the therapist to ask clients if their descriptions seem to fit.

The following is a transcript of part of a session in which a 16-year-old daughter was on probation and continued to get positive results on a drug test for marijuana. As the daughter was able to make other changes in her life, her stand against marijuana became easier.

Therapist 1: (To Therapist 2) Hmmm! I'm impressed with the stand she is willing to take against impatience.

T2:   (To T1) Me too. Most people really struggle with impatience, usually just giving in.

T1:   Yes, you see impatience everywhere. On the highway coming over here, receptionists putting me on hold. . . .

T2:   Waiting for spring to come. . . .

T1:   (To teenage daughter) Listening to all the stories about how you have struggled with impatience over time, how were you ever able to stand in line for 45 minutes to get your driving license?

Desiree: I had to do it, so I just did it.

T1:   (To T2) I wonder what this could mean?

T2:   (To T1) One possibility is that Desiree is becoming more impatient with obstacles that have been imposed on her life because of drug use.

T1:   Hmm, very interesting. Placing the impatience where it belongs, against the problem.

T2:   (Back to Desiree) In what other areas of your life do you find yourself becoming more tolerant?

Desiree: Ummm, my brother. We didn't fight that much this week.

If You Want to Get Their Attention, Whisper

When working with chaotic systems, overtalking and side conversations can burst into conflagrations rather quickly. Frequently, in early sessions, chaos leads to blame, personal attack, and, of course, shouting. Families will indeed experience hopelessness, disempowerment, and shame when therapy sessions turn sour in this way. The importance of having good breaks to apply during such anarchy cannot be emphasized enough.

Cotherapists can lean subtly toward one another and, in a low speaking voice, reframe the discord as, perhaps, "Hmmm, this family certainly seems to have megatons of energy to get this problem out of their home once and for all." As long as the process is interrupted promptly, the family members will all turn toward the therapists to listen in on what the therapists could possibly be talking about. A brief conversation could follow, speculating on readiness for change, guessing who might be willing to take the first step toward change, or wondering how the family was able to generate such energy in preparation to take action against the problem.

The discourse may likely take on the themes of caring, perseverance, unity, strength, or love. Depending on what model of family therapy the team is using, the session can more successfully be taken from there.

T1:   (To T2 in a low tone) I am encouraged by the energy that all the family members are showing to make themselves heard.

T2:   (To T1 in a low tone) Yes. They seem to care enough that others in the family know what they are thinking and feeling.

T1:   (To T2 in a low tone) I am wondering how we can help them to use this persistence to address their concerns.

T2:   (To T1 in normal tone) Let's ask them.

Building a Metaphor

The family therapy field is loaded with indexes of literature on how the client's use of metaphors give us clues about how they see the world and how they could move themselves into healthier, more satisfying relationships together (Rosenblatt, 1994). Families use metaphors in a variety of ways to describe their dilemmas, their past, their dynamics, and the structure of their system. The therapeutic team can also capitalize on these metaphors to evoke lasting change. Often metaphors are obscure, and as some might say, four ears are better than two. One cotherapist may catch a metaphor that the other therapist missed because metaphors are often disguised in everyday conversation. The therapist who noticed the analogic blurb can quickly relate it, tying it together with the family's goals, using gossip. For example, a recent intake session involved a couple's problems with overinvolved in-laws, ex-spouse interference, and difficulties solving problems together without dramatic arguments. After hearing some of this story, the therapists began filling out the basic forms in the clients' chart, providing an opening for gossip from the start of the session.

T1:   Address?
Larry: 105 Mountain Avenue, Springport.
T1:   Phone?
Larry: 555-6664.
T1:   Insurance information?
Larry: Do you have the card, dear?
Martha: Yes, here it is.
T1:   Thanks. . . . Occupation?
Larry: Actually, I'm self-employed. I run heavy equipment to build agricultural fences.
T2:   Building fences?
Larry: Yup.
Martha: And I handle the books. He'd have trouble staying in business if it weren't for what I do with the books.
T2:   (Toward T1) That's great!
T1:   (Turning toward T2) Huh?
T2:   Well, since Larry is already an expert on building fences, they may have an advantage at reclaiming their privacy.
T1:   Yes, and if Martha is keen in attention to details, just think, we may get to the bottom line much quicker.

After this brief dialogue, the couple entered therapy with the anticipation of having an advanced level of mastery necessary to work toward solutions collaboratively. Literature on using metaphor in family work is vast, and readers are encouraged to explore material connecting to their preferred model of therapy.

Split Team "Both/And" Gossip

Yalom (1985) surveyed 20 patients about the effect of in-session cotherapist disagreement and its effect on the progress of their psychotherapy groups. All 20 believed it was beneficial to their professional growth. The phenomenon was explained as a model-setting experience, in which two professionals, experts in communication, could disagree openly and come to some resolve with dignity and respect. When working systemically, this effect can be taken a bit further (as in the Mental Research Institute model). Couples or families can be placed in a therapeutic double bind as the co-therapy team is torn between two opposing viewpoints. The therapists, in this case, can agree and disagree at the same time. When this happens, clients have the room to compare their experience to that of the cotherapy team members and come to a new reality of their situations.

The following dialogue is with a husband recovering from a cocaine addiction that was destroying his marriage and his depressed wife who had disengaged herself from therapy because of her skepticism about his recovery. The wife was prompted to participate again in therapy when the male therapist invited a female cotherapist to join the sessions. The couple was at an impasse.

T1:   (To T2) Mr. Jones seems to want to work on his sobriety and stay away from drugs.

T2:   (To T1) That may be so, but I see a strong desire for him to socialize with his previous drug-using friends.

T1:   (To T2) Yes, that's true. I wonder which is going to win, his friends or his marriage.

T2:   (To T1) Let's check with him to see which one has the upper hand.

Children and Adolescents

Rule number 1 in working with children or adolescents is to be mindful of the developmental level of the client. Children can be especially open to gossip. More than one mother has said in session, "Be careful. They pick up on everything." Gossiping can be a way of talking to children or adolescents without addressing them directly. This is helpful when the person is withdrawn or rebellious.

Strategic Gossip

Resistance can be side-stepped with strategic gossip. As with all strategic therapy, important rules should be applied to strategic intervention. As you read the following dialogue, keep these two guidelines in mind: The directive must fit the client, and it cannot lead them into harm's way.

When recently questioning a 12-year-old girl with a habit of running away from home on a frequent basis, a male–female cotherapy team asked her how she came to the decision not to let anybody know she was only staying with a cousin for 5 days. She responded, "I don't know." After rephrasing the question in several different ways, the girl became rather frustrated, and her best response was "It just sort of got blanked out." At this point one therapist turned to the other and said:

T1:   Uh-oh . . . This could be much more serious than I first thought.
T2:   I was thinking the same thing.
T1:   I hope it's not . . . but this could be very serious.
T2:   If it's amnesia or some kind of trance she goes into, could it happen at any time? Could she really be such a danger to herself? Maybe even get hit by a car?
T1:   I guess we have to report this . . . children in danger and all . . . maybe short-term hospitalization.

At this point the girl interrupted and explained the details of how she came to the decision not to call in. Her explanation led to a larger picture of how the system interacted and how change could be built.

Termination

On reaching their initial goals and launching new plans, the family will get a taste of empowerment and may invite the therapists to take the therapy a bit further. After several successful sessions, members may test newly claimed territories and risk airing some emotionally charged issues, especially as a family member or spouse visits some symptom perhaps never before mentioned in therapy. This provides a difficult clinical decision for the therapist who is mindful of time constraints mandated by private or public funding agencies.

This scenario also provides an opportunity to gossip. First, however, the cotherapists sit back and observe the process as the family interacts around this heated issue. Hoping the process does not escalate, the team watches for the family's use of respect, sensitivity, or other goals that they may have worked so hard on in their initial treatment plan. Once the conversation seems to be going successfully, perhaps after 10 minutes, the cotherapy team can begin the gossip even as the family is still talking. The team, in their dialogue, can discuss with each other all of the qualities of interaction they observed with the family. They can question each other about what these developments could mean. The conclusion that the therapists ultimately reach is how they may no longer be needed by the family to iron out all the difficulties they brought to the therapy.

T1:   Hmm.
T2:   Wow.
T1:   I don't know whether to be surprised or not.
T2:   I was just watching this.
T1:   The overtalking has virtually stopped.
T2:   Not only that, did you see Justin looking so interested in what everybody had to say before giving his response?
T1:   Yes, that's a far cry from when we first started.
T2:   When we first started he didn't even want to stay in that chair.
T1:   And Aunt Sheila, did you see how she backed out, declining the invitation to give advice at every chance?
T2:   Yes, and Mom was really engaged in talking to Justin like I've never seen before.
T1:   I wonder if they all could tell us what they were doing differently this evening?
T2:   If they can, I wonder what this means about how long they are going to need us?
T1:   Well, let's find out.

Single-Therapist Format

Almost any gossiping technique can be used in a single-therapist format. When used in this way, gossiping is an overt expression of the thoughts and feelings of the therapist that she or he wishes to communicate to the family. This is a powerful technique when the therapist is attempting to relay a dual description (two different ways of describing the same dynamics) or a feeling of being torn between two different directions to go in therapy.

In working with a family who had a boy in placement with the Department of Social Services for intermittent explosive disorder and oppositional defiant disorder, this technique came in handy in exploring options about what direction to take in therapy and how soon the boy should be returned home.

T: Who would be the least surprised by yours and Steven's marvelous development attained so far in therapy?

Dad: Well. I don't know. Steven seems to always get better after a short time in placement. But soon after he comes home, it's the same old thing. Steven's problem comes back and then some.

T: Hmmm. (Pause) Pardon me while I think this one over. Part of me says the problem may indeed come back, yet I heard evidence of two parents willing to do something differently if things don't go well. On the other hand, I heard Steven arguing for the chance to restrain the problem before his father has to do it. . . . I need a minute to think. . . . Well, Steven, let me ask you this: On a scale of 1 to 10, with 10 being completely ready to go back home and 1 being totally not ready to go home, where do you see yourself?

Steven: A 6.

T: What do you think you need to do differently to get to a 7?

Steven: The cussing. Got to stop the cussing.

T: What would be a good cuss word for a 7?

Another method the therapist could use to gossip when working alone is to use a telephone. Some family therapy rooms are already equipped with phones; if not, a cellular phone or home phone (for home-based therapy) can come in handy. It is best to ask the family for permission to take a break to call your colleague, cotherapist, or clinical supervisor for their thoughts about the family's dilemma. If no one can be reached, it is acceptable to call your own voice mail, weather service, or recorded stock reports. When the colleague, or service, answers the phone the therapist can run through events that led the family to the place where the therapist felt stuck. The therapist then asks over the phone for several ideas for the family to get through this dilemma. The retelling of the story to the colleague, whether there is another colleague on the phone or not, often refreshes the therapist's view of what is going on with this family. It even provides the therapist some valuable time to figure out where he or she was led astray and how to refocus in the moment. As the family listens carefully, the therapist could reframe details (from a positive viewpoint), talk about the family's picture using language from structural family therapy, or comment on power metaphors. This phone break provides the opportunity to launch techniques from whatever model the therapist chooses. As the therapist listens to a recorded message or a live colleague, he or she can formulate a number of questions that may get the family and the therapist back on track.

Conclusion

One basic rule in the use of gossip is to be mindful of overuse. It can be an enjoyable technique for both clients and therapists. Overuse of the technique, as with any technique, could diminish its potency. Some families could feel unimportant, as if they were not even in the room, or they could get bored when the therapists break into long conversations at every possible moment. Used sparingly, a little gossip goes a long way.

Some adults appreciate and prefer directness and could see the gossiping as a sort of performance. By attending to any nonverbal reactions of the family members during the gossip, an intermediate practitioner should be able to detect any animosity or dissonance from a family member against the team. Keep in mind, no response is a response in itself. Therapeutic gossip is a rather advanced technique and requires a degree of skill and practice. This technique is most safely used when the dialogue between the therapists feels natural and not scripted. One final caveat: Care should be taken to assure the gossip fits the culture of the family.

References

Andersen, T. (Ed.). (1991). *The reflecting team: Dialogues and dialogues about the dialogues*. New York: Norton.

Knight, C. (1990). Use of support groups with adult female survivors of child sexual abuse. *Social Work, 35*, 202–206.

Rosenblatt, P. C. (1994). *Metaphors of family systems therapy*. New York: Guilford Press.

White, M. (1993). Deconstruction and therapy. In S. Gilligan & R. Price (Eds.), *Therapeutic conversations* (pp. 22–61). New York: Norton. (Reprinted from *Dulwich Centre Newsletter, 3*, pp. 1–22, 1991)

Yalom, I. D. (1985). *The theory and practice of group psychotherapy*. New York: Basic Books.

PART

APPENDIX

Appendix **A**

The How I Remember My Family Questionnaire

Please answer the following questions based on your childhood memories of your family. Please do not write on this sheet.

Your Father

1. How would you describe your father? How would you describe his personality style?
2. How would you describe your relationship to him?
3. In what ways are you similar to your father? In what ways are your different?

Your Mother

1. How would you describe your mother? How would you describe her personality style?
2. How would you describe your relationship to her?
3. In what ways are you similar to your mother? In what ways are you different?

Your Parents' Marriage

1. How would you describe your parents' view of their roles and responsibilities as husband and wife? Was one partner more dominant or was it a fairly equal relationship? What is your overall impression of their relationship?
2. What was the decision-making process? That is, how were decisions made and who usually made them?

3. How would you describe the communication between your parents in their marital relationship?

4. How was marital conflict handled?

5. How did your parents manage finances?

6. What was the division of labor in managing the home, possessions, social life, vacations, and the like?

7. How did your parents relate to extended family members (in-laws, other relatives, and close family friends)?

8. How did your parents view human sexuality? How was intimacy and sexuality understood and expressed in their relationship?

9. How did your parents address the subject of religion?

10. What impact did your father's and mother's vocations have on their marital relationship?

11. What aspects of your parents' marriage do you want to incorporate into your marriage? Why? (Be sure to check your responses to questions 1–8 above.)

12. What aspects of your parents' marriage do you want to avoid? Why? (Be sure to check your responses to questions 1–8 above.)

Your Parents as Parents

1. How did your parents feel about having children? Do you want children? Why or why not? How is your perspective of children similar or different to that of your parents? How is it different?

2. Describe your parents' parenting style. That is, describe your parents as parents. Were they in agreement on how the children should be reared? Please explain your answer.

3. What aspects of their parenting style do your want to incorporate into your family? Why?

4. What aspects of their parenting style do you want to avoid? Why?

Your Siblings

1. How many brothers and sisters do you have? In what order were they born?

2. How would you describe your brother(s) when you were children? How would you describe him/them now?

3. How would you describe your sister(s) when you were children? How would you describe her/them now?

4. Which of your siblings are you most like? Please explain.

5. Which of your siblings are you most unlike? Please explain.

■ ■ ■